Golf Has Never Failed Me

The Lost Commentaries of Legendary Golf Architect Donald J. Ross

Sleeping Bear Press   Sleeping Bear Ltd.
121 South Main St.   12 Chauntry Road
P.O. Box 20   Bray, Maidenhead
Chelsea, MI 48118   Berkshire, England

Printed in the United States of America

10 9 8 7 6 5 4 3 2 1

Library of Congress CIP Data on File

Golf Has Never Failed Me

The Lost Commentaries of Legendary Golf Architect Donald J. Ross

Contents

Foreword

My father once told me he approached every new course with the idea that the golf player, champion or duffer, should complete his round challenged by the layout and enriched by the beauty of nature.

I recall his redesigning an entire hole at the Ponkapoag Golf Club in Massachusetts just to save one beautiful tree. At Pinehurst, the old No. 6 hole—the Cathedral hole—on what was then the No. 3 course, with its approach over water to the green, surrounded by pink and white dogwood and backed by Cathedral pines, was a feast for the inner man. In our home he always brought to the dinner table a choice rose, freshly clipped from his carefully tended rose gardens.

Donald Ross was a wise, especially gentle and devoted father to me, his only child. His reverence for nature, dedication to keeping the game the finest he knew, and his great sympathy for players of all abilities, made him the ideal architect for the golfing world.

Now to all of you who love the game, my father's own words bring an understanding of how he worked to leave such an unforgettable legacy.

Lillian Ross Pippitt

When I was a young man in Scotland, I read about America and the American businessman absorbed in making money. I knew the day would come when the American businessman would relax and want some game to play, and I knew that game would be golf. I read about the start of golf in the United States, and knew there would be a great future in it, so I learned all I could about the game: teaching, playing, clubmaking, greenkeeping and course construction. And then I came to America to grow up with a game in which I had complete confidence.

Golf has never failed me.

Donald J. Ross.

Introduction

The Legend
We Hardly Know

THE ESTABLISHED IMAGE of America's all-time favorite golf architect, Donald J. Ross, is a kindly, white-haired grandfather, in his three-piece suit and wire-rimmed glasses, a proper gentleman who, from his home base in Pinehurst, sketched out sterling golf course plans that have been the venues of the finest championships in the game.

We golfers may think we know Donald Ross from playing his many courses and studying golf history books. But there's much we don't know about him.

Ross was both a playing and teaching professional, but by 1910 he had made golf course architecture his primary occupation. Within ten years, Donald Ross had become the first superstar of American golf.

Granted, he did not have the glittery array of medals that Bobby Jones collected, or the swashbuckling charm that Walter Hagen exuded, or the youthful showmanship that Gene Sarazen displayed, but in a time when Hagen and Sarazen were playing for total purses of just one thousand dollars, Donald Ross was making $30,000 a year designing golf courses.

He assembled a talented team of assistants and was the first to tack the term "associates" onto his letter-head. He had winter offices at Pinehurst, North Carolina, a summer office in Little Compton, Rhode Island, and branch offices in Chicago, Massachusetts and Pennsylvania. In 1925, it was estimated that 3,000 men were employed in the construction and mainte-nance of his various courses.

His name was a designer label and appeared in advertisements for resort courses, calendars, grass seed and other turf products. He designed a set of signature golf clubs, produced by Bristol Golf Equipment.

As an accomplished tournament player, he won two Massachusetts Opens, placed eighth place in the 1910 British Open at St. Andrews and competed in seven U.S. Opens, finishing in the top 10 four times.

He is considered the most prolific architect in history, with well over 400 courses, all done in an age when travel consisted of arduous automobile or train trips. His fans don't really know how many golf courses Donald Ross designed and remodeled in his 48-year career. Ross once admitted he'd lost count, but in 1935 he could remember doing something in 45 of 48 states, excepting only Arizona, Utah, and Montana. If that's true, some of his courses have been lost to the ages.

He was inventive in areas besides design. He is cred-ited with creating the first indoor golf school in Amer-ica, in Boston, soon after he arrived in the United States. He also created the first practice and lesson tee, the famous "Maniac Hill" at Pinehurst.

No architect in his day had more influence on his craft. When Ross really started devoting his energies to

The name Donald J. Ross was a designer label for everything from clubs to courses.

golf architecture in 1910, the job was still considered to be that primarily of an engineer. The competition at the time—C.B. MacDonald, Devereux Emmet, Willie Park, Jr.—were competent at superimposing golf holes onto sites, but the results were startlingly artificial.

Ross transformed golf design into an art form and the profession into one for an artist. He produced marvelous routing plans that merged golf holes comfortably into the landscape. The small details were as important to Ross as the grand design, especially the finesse shots around the greens. Anyone who has played Pinehurst No. 2 would surely agree.

Ross had a wry humor about his architecture. "It has been my good fortune to bring happiness to many men," he told his audience at a 1930 testimonial dinner, "and great trouble to many men."

Ross also was one of the first to convert sand greens to grass. After one ten-hour day in the heat at Pinehurst he said, "I was plastered with dust, and looked like a coal miner."

Admirers today tend to stereotype his architecture: Always crowned greens. Never sand flashed against a bunker face. Always an open approach into the green. Never a bunker behind the green.

But Donald Ross was much more imaginative than that. In today's terms, he was "site-specific" in his work. When the location called for it, he'd tuck a green down into a hollow and surround it with perched bunkers. In pure sand, he built sweeping sand dune bunkers with faces as bold as anything at Merion. When the approach called for a short-iron pitch, he'd sometimes clutter the front of the green with terrifying hazards. He liked the occasional surprise beyond the flag, be it a bunker, a mound or hollow.

We know less about the true architecture of Donald

Ross than we'd like because most of his courses have changed in the half century since his death, as every golf course is in a state of constant evolution.

In the post-war euphoria of automatic irrigation, electric carts and lively balls, a good portion of the Donald Ross philosophy of architecture got bulldozed away and grassed over. The game of golf is poorer for that. So is our true understanding of Donald Ross.

It didn't help that Ross was the least published golf architect of his day. His competitors, especially A.W. Tillinghast, William S. Flynn, Alister MacKenzie, H.S. Colt, Perry Maxwell and Max Behr, all wrote extensively about their architecture in magazines, pamphlets and books.

Only recently did a Donald Ross manuscript resurface. Written before World War I, it was intended to be published in 1914 but for reasons we will never know, it was never published. After Ross' death, it was in the possession of his long-time associate J.B. McGovern and it found its way recently to the American Society of Golf Course Architects and the Ross family.

That manuscript forms the basis for this book. To do complete justice to Donald Ross, the manuscript has been edited and supplemented with other commentaries made by Ross during his career.

The result is the definitive work of Donald J. Ross, a book of far-reaching content. Most of Donald Ross' observations regarding golf still hold true today. There is prescience in some of his comments, irony in other statements, and his wry humor in still others. There is old-fashioned common sense in all of them.

The aim of this book is to present the words of Donald Ross as if he himself had edited it toward the twilight of his career. The pages deal not only with his ground rules of golf design, but also his views on the other aspects of golf.

You will meet a legend in these pages.

What follows is pure Donald Ross, in his own words, reflecting upon the game that never failed him.

Ron Whitten
Architectural Editor
Golf Digest

My Reasons Why

OF ALL THE DELIGHTFUL, helpful books written about golf, don't you think it's rather striking that there has never been a book published in this country on the scientific laying out and building of courses? The architecture of golf, if you please.

To take our cue for laying out courses in this country by what has been done in England is hardly fair, as climatic conditions, length of days and playing opportunities are radically different over there.

In both England and Scotland it rains frequently, practically every week. It's a drought if it doesn't. Grass fairly revels under such conditions. In halfway favorable soil, you can be assured of ideal results.

Here, where it often does not rain for several weeks and courses are swept by drying winds, the problem is entirely different and distinctly difficult.

England's summer days are so much longer than ours that a businessman can take a run on the train after work for an hour and a half out to the links, have dinner and still be able to play eighteen holes in abundant light. That makes it possible to select locations for links that have the natural condition of the soil and lay of the ground in their favor.

Our days are so short and the time of our businessmen so limited that our courses must be located where quickly accessible.

Generally, such available ground has few natural conditions in its favor, so courses must be laid out and molded in ways to impart the essential zest and intent to the game.

It is this side of golf, then, that I am going to talk over with you.

Many of my friends who have played on the famed links constructed under my supervision at Pinehurst, North Carolina, have urged me over and over again to be a "wee bit" generous and put in available book form some of my "reasons why" for the laying out of golf courses and handling of golf course problems.

So I am going to do it, in my offhand way, just like you and I were sitting before the fire some evening, talking it over while accompanied by the soulful solace of a friendly pipe.

How I Got My Start

I WILL BEGIN BY ANSWERING a question I'm often asked: How did I get my start?

It's very peculiar. You see, when I got through my schooling I became a carpenter by trade and worked where I lived, up in Dornoch in the Highlands. I belonged to the golf club and played there, and finally the members came to feel that they needed a professional at Dornoch, someone to make clubs and give lessons.

In those days, you see, golf clubs all were made by hand. Now they are modeled and turned out by machines, but there were no machines for such things back then. Anyway, they thought I would be the person for the job, being a carpenter, I suppose. So I went to St. Andrews for a year and Carnoustie for another, to learn the trade. And then I came home and took up the position.

I also became the greenkeeper, although we didn't dignify the task by any such title. What I really did was to go out in overalls and get down on my hands and knees, and care for the turf and the bunkers and the greens. And how I used to hate it. But, as it turned out, that was the best training I could have had for what turned out to be my future.

Well, sir, one time a professor, Robert Willson of

Harvard University, came to Dornoch and after he had played a few times he approached me and explained that golf was just beginnning to catch hold in America, and that they needed some one to teach the game and promote it. He asked how I would like to come over to America.

Your author, shortly after his arrival in the states, back at the turn of the century.

I said I hadn't given the matter much thought, but when he said that I could make $60 a month and I would get fifty cents an hour for lessons, I began to think about it. You see, that was three times what I was making in Dornoch. Although, when I told my mother about the idea of going to America, she said I had the best job in town, which I had, and why should I give it up? I was making £100 a year where I was. That's $500. Still, I thought I might be able to do better in this country. So I accepted the offer.

Well, I never shall forget the day I arrived in New York. After paying for my passage I had very little money left, and I had to figure how to get to Boston. I looked up the fare and saw I would have enough with a few shillings left over, so I walked all the way from the boat to the Grand Central Station. But then I made the mistake of getting on an extra-fare train.

I was practically flat broke when I reached Boston, but I called up Mr. Willson on the telephone and he told me to come right out and stay with him. I certainly was glad to hear him say that. But I walked all the way from Boston to Cambridge so I would have a little money left.

The next day I went out to look at the Oakley course where I was to work. It was covered with snow. It looked like an impossible problem. But I went to work on it with fifty men and that year I sent $2,000 home to my mother in Dornoch.

And that's how I got started.

My Design Standards

THESE ARE MY STANDARDS to laying out a golf course:

Make each hole present a different problem.

So arrange it that every stroke must be made with a full concentration and attention necessary to good golf.

Build each hole in such a manner that it wastes none of the ground at my disposal, and takes advantage of every possibility I can see.

Stop Throwing Stones

STOP THROWING STONES at the chairman of the green committee! He is doing what he believes to be best. It's the rest of you who are to blame. You can't censure a captain who runs his ship onto sandbars if you don't give him a chart to steer by.

Right there lies half the clubs' troubles of today. They have no chart to go by. Let me tell you exactly what I mean by no chart.

A chairman of the green committee has pretty much all the say of what work shall be done on the course each year. He locates the placement of new bunkers, directs the changing of tees, advises as to what shall be done on the care of the putting greens, and does whatever else seems consistent to him for the improvement of the course.

The following year a new chairman is elected, and he starts putting his own ideas in force. Many of them may be directly opposite from those of his predecessor. Bunkers are ripped out and new ones made, new tees are built, and new methods used in the care of greens. All are done under the direction of a man lacking in experience but anxious to try out his own individual ideas.

The club pays for all this.

And this kind of thing goes on year after year, in greater or lesser degree, in every club in this big, glad country of ours.

Sometimes it becomes so serious that factions are formed with all their attendant, unfortunate, disrupting results.

Over in England they do these things better. They have a paid secretary, who continues in office year after year. He handles the course on a definite plan. He is working toward certain well-defined results. There is a continuity of purpose in his work.

Over there, the green committee acts as a board of directors. A policy is outlined and strictly adhered to, just like in any business.

Is there any reason why such a system could not be adopted in America?

Over and over again, it has been the history of clubs in this country that where one man has been in authority, working on lines laid down by a definite plan, the course has improved wonderfully and continues to improve.

It is also a noticeable fact that employees do their work better and at less cost when keeping in touch with such a continued authority.

Why is it that shrewd men, who recognize it is vital in their business to have a well-defined policy and demand adherence to it, sanction the very opposite action when it comes to golf club matters?

Courses should be laid out by an expert, the plan submitted to the green committee and agreed upon. This plan should in turn be thoroughly understood and passed upon by the club as a whole. Then this plan becomes the chart for all future operations of the club.

Individual ideas cannot have sway. One man, or a favored few who contribute largely to the support of any club, cannot dominate things.

The adopted plan must be abided by.

This effectual method applies to the control of old courses quite as much as to ones about to be laid out.

Call in an expert golf architect. What if it does cost real money? It will save the club many dollars in the end, and go a long way toward preserving that unity of feeling so vital for the success and continued pleasure of any golf club.

Location, Location, Location

Naturally, one of the first considerations in selecting a site for a golf course is convenience in transportation facilities. But happily, in this age of automobiles, we can tolerate a little inconvenience in favor of some other equally important requirement. So soil conditions should be of very first importance.

A sandy loam is by far the very best golfing soil.

It provides good drainage and ideal conditions for strong, enduring growth of desirable grasses. It likewise furnishes the exact conditions necessary for the proper playing of golf strokes.

Such a soil on a putting green gives the cushion so essential for a pitched ball. Such a stroke can never be quite as satisfactory when played on any other soil condition.

Bunkering on a sandy soil can be done scientifically, for you are providing the player with conditions that justify your demand of a more skillful stroke.

One other thing highly in favor of such a soil is that you can play on it both early and late in the season. After rains, it is not slippery, is quickly drained, and

From the tee of the fourth at Pine Needles in North Carolina, a most delightful terrain.

becomes playable. During the hot months it will not bake.

By sandy, I mean a soil containing very little of the necessary plant food in the form of humus. With the introduction of a humus or compost, such soil provides delightful conditions.

Of all the land I've surveyed for courses, none compares to the sand barrens around Pinehurst, NC.

Some notable examples of such conditions are to be found on courses laid out on Long Island. Equally satisfactory conditions can also be found in the vicinity of Cape Cod in Massachusetts, where there are sand dunes galore, furnishing that undulating variety so welcomed by golfing enthusiasts.

Another superb location: Plainfield (NJ) Country Club, with gently flowing hills where golf holes can roll across the landscape.

In traveling on Lake Shore Road approaching Chicago, I have frequently noticed what appears to be ideal golfing country.

There's great individuality in each golf course, and you can't really compare two layouts; for instance,

Oyster Harbors in Massachusetts and Waterbury in Connecticut. The soil and terrain are so different.

But give me some slightly rolling terrain and sandy soil, and I'll give you the best courses.

Locations To Be Avoided

SOILS OF A CLAY MIXTURE are to be avoided if possible.

They are difficult to drain and must be given much costly attention to produce satisfactory turf. They are continually muddy and slippery in the early and late seasons. During the hot months, they are hard and baked. After rains they are apt to be overrun with worms.

Their playing conditions are exceedingly inconsistent, as they vary according to the weather. If it's a dry Monday, the course is too dry. If it's a wet Tuesday, it's too wet. And so it goes. It's absolutely undependable.

The grass winter-kills badly and the bunkers, if not carefully drained, are little less than mud pits.

In some sections, however, a clay soil is the only one available.

In such cases you must simply make up your mind to accept the limitations of such a course and be prepared to cheerfully and continually spend money for its up-keep and betterment.

Unfortunately, such soils are found near a large portion of our major cities.

In New England, rocky sites can't be avoided. It takes skill to chisel holes such as the eighth at Charles River Country Club near Boston.

A Course Divided is No Course

BEFORE DECIDING UPON any piece of property, make sure it is going to lay out to your advantage.

Unless absolutely necessary, don't for a minute consider a property divided by either a street or a railroad.

The very intent of a golf course is to get away from just such things.

It causes annoyance to both members and those using the road, and often brings the public and club members into conflict. It always means the undesirable division of your course in at least two units, and often more. This means a separate problem for each division and very often, because of their limitations, prevents the taking advantage of natural conditions.

All of which means greater expense in laying out the course.

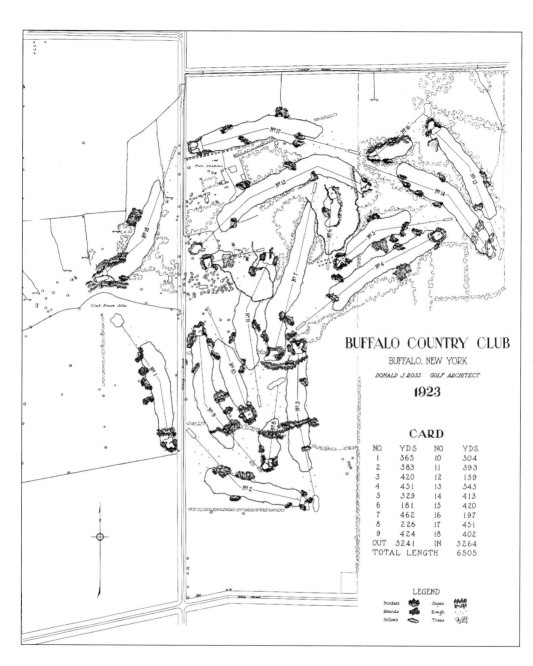

BUFFALO COUNTRY CLUB

BUFFALO, NEW YORK

DONALD J. ROSS   GOLF ARCHITECT

1923

CARD

NO.	YDS	NO	YDS.
1	365	10	304
2	383	11	393
3	420	12	139
4	451	13	545
5	329	14	413
6	181	15	420
7	462	16	197
8	226	17	451
9	424	18	402
OUT	3241	IN	3264
TOTAL LENGTH			6505

LEGEND

Bunkers		Slopes	
Mounds		Rough	
Hollows		Trees	

An exception to the rule. The road running through the Country Club of Buffalo (NY) barely interfered with the natural progression of holes.

24

Good and Bad Shapes

ONE OF THE DESIRABLE SHAPES for a piece of golfing property is that of a fan. It gives you an opportunity to place your clubhouse at the handle of the fan and then lay out two loops of nine holes each on either side from it. The first tee, ninth green, tenth tee and eighteenth green are then all at the handle of the fan near the clubhouse.

Those who desire to play nine holes can then be accommodated without cutting in. When the course is crowded, players can start at either the first or the tenth tees, which greatly relieves congestion.

Such a division of the course affords another rather pleasing feature, as members can stop after nine, have refreshments and rest if desired.

An oblong shape also works out to splendid advantage, as you can place the clubhouse near the center boundary line and lay out nine holes on both sides.

A square tract of land is hard to handle, as there are almost certain to be losses in the corners. It presents many difficult problems in securing a satisfactory layout, particularly if the tract is limited in size.

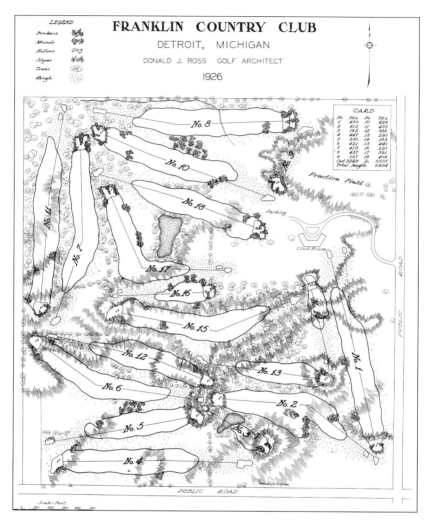

Franklin Hills (MI) Country Club is a fine fan-shaped routing on a rectangular tract that neither wastes nor compromises the land.

How Much Land Is Needed?

DON'T MAKE THAT MOST regrettable of mistakes, the selection of too small a tract. Don't try to save money in that way. One hundred ten acres will do, but it's bad to limit it to even that. One hundred twenty-five is a fair size, but one hundred fifty is by far better.

It is not necessary for clubs to use all the ground available for golf. By using less, the upkeep is kept down, a big item in this day of high prices.

Under certain favorable conditions, a small piece of property, fortunately shaped, might work out admirably. Other times, it would make a most unsatisfactory and decidedly uninteresting course.

This is another undebatable reason why you should call upon the assistance of an expert and be guided by his advice in the selection of your land.

By an expert, mind you, I mean an expert—not a golf enthusiast, who feels himself an expert—but an expert golf architect who is also a golf enthusiast.

Protect Your Club

BUY THE LAND.

The very day your club decides to rent a piece of land, that same day its value and that of all surrounding land immediately increases.

Real estate men, recognizing this, are quick to snap up all available nearby property.

So buy your land at the start if you can. If you don't, then rent for a term of years with the absolute privilege of purchase at the end of the term for a definite specified sum.

Protect your club.

Don't be like one I have in mind that could have reserved the privilege of buying its property for $300 an acre less than six years ago. Now the owner is demanding $3000 an acre. Furthermore, the property is now worth it.

Design on Land, Not on Paper

WHEN ENGAGED TO LAY OUT A COURSE, I visit the land and walk over it until I have a complete grasp of the conditions and possibilities of the tract.

This is first done without any attempt to lay out the course. It may take two days or more to accomplish this, depending entirely on the extent and the nature of the property.

After going over it in this fashion, I then select all the good holes possible, irrespective of whether they shall be in the final layout.

One can find on almost any tract a few attractive golfing situations that should be taken advantage of. In the final layout, I include all of those selected holes that I possibly can.

It has always seemed to me better to have a few very fine holes and the rest fair, than eighteen fair holes with none that leave a distinct impression on the player's mind. Such a course can never be attractive as a playing proposition as it soon ceases to bait the player. It becomes stale to club members.

Each tract has its own problems. Each offers its own

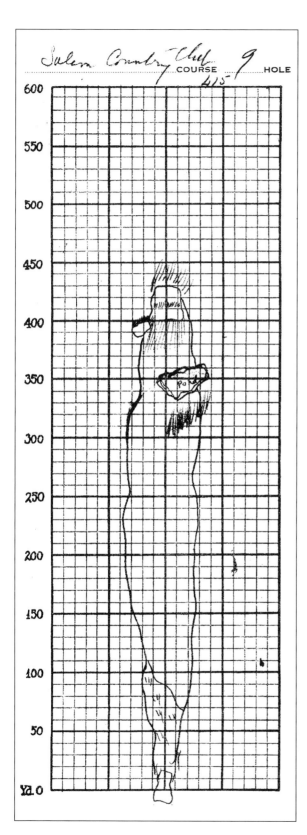

Once the concept of a hole is determined, it is reduced to a scale drawing from which it can be faithfully constructed.

The finished ninth at Salem Country Club, Peabody, MA, was built in accordance with its diagram.

opportunities. Take advantage of the opportunities, and you may secure holes with distinct interest that will furnish a constant joy to those who play them.

Nowadays, golf architects must be first-class landscape gardeners. The idea is to mold nature just sufficiently to give the greatest golf possibilities.

Until you are thoroughly familiar with the topographical formation of a property and the golfing possibilities presented, it is absolutely futile to attempt laying out a course on paper. However, there are certain fundamental ideas that can govern the laying out of any course. Let's you and I talk them over together in their broadest sense.

Each Course Must Be Original

A COURSE THAT CONTINUALLY OFFERS PROBLEMS—one with fight in it, if you please—is the one that keeps the player keen for the game.

Take, for example, the Old Course at St. Andrews, Scotland, which is more often played by Americans than any other course in Europe. Who, after playing it, can forget such holes as the eleventh or seventeenth, with their subtleties, charm and never-ceasing allurement?

Surely no one can forget the feeling of joy after placing his second shot on the plateau greens on the fourth or eighth at Dornoch, my old home course, one of the best and most enjoyable courses in the world.

Courses have become famous merely because they have one or two holes which stand out in the memory of the players as supreme tests for the golfer.

But don't let famed holes like those or many others, such as the "Alps" of Prestwick and "Redan" of North Berwick, lead you into attempting to reproduce them. In trying to make your course fit certain famous hole

The eleventh green at the South course of Oakland Hills Country Club, Bloomfield Hills, MI, was fit into a natural saddle between two hills.

treatments, you are certain to be doomed to disappointment.

Make your holes fit your course. No other way can be as satisfactory.

Each Course Must Have Strategies

THE DESIGN OF AMERICAN COURSES in the early days of golf differed materially from the practices of this age.

Tees were built up two feet above ground level and were framed with wood, appearing like cigar boxes set in the ground.

Greens were twice as large as they are now, and all were square in shape.

Bunkers were square symmetrical "cops," or hills, placed directly across the line of play.

Designers followed the idea of penalizing the poor player. He had to drive into the bunkers or over them.

Today, strategy governs the game to a large extent. The golfer can escape the bunkers, but he loses distance thereby. Emphasis today is laid upon punishing the proficient player.

In laying out a course, the cardinal rule is to make the holes so that the man who plays it as he should gets par, and the man who makes a mistake makes one more than par.

In building my courses, my aim is to lay out an alternate route on practically every hole. That is, in the case

An early-day tee box atop timbers, yet a periscope was still needed to see the fairway. Such contrivances must be avoided.

of a two-shot hole, the scratch player or long hitter has one way of getting home in two shots—he must place his drive accurately to do so—and the high handicapper or short hitter has another route to reach the green in three.

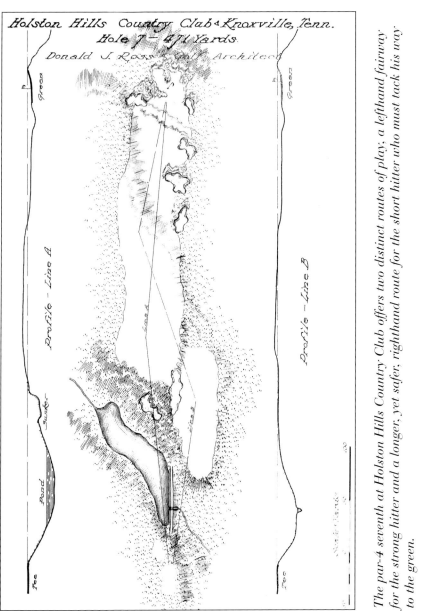

The par-4 seventh at Holston Hills Country Club offers two distinct routes of play; a lefthand fairway for the strong hitter and a longer, yet safer, righthand route for the short hitter who must tack his way to the green.

The Ideal Course

THE IDEAL COURSE IS one that presents a test of golf for the everyday golfer and the first-class player.

A properly designed course can take care of every class of golfer.

My aim is to bring out of the player the best golf that is in him.

It will be difficult to negotiate some holes, but that is what golf is for.

It is a mental test and an eye test.

The hazards and bunkers are placed so as to force a man to use judgment and to exercise mental control in making the correct shot.

Where to Put the Clubhouse

THE RIGHT LOCATION for the clubhouse is vital.

Not only should it be directly adjacent to the starting point of the course, but it should be placed so that the avenue reaching it does not cut across any portion of the course.

There should be a rear access for the deliveries and other essential activities that should be kept decidedly in the background. The caddie shack should be placed so that its proximity to the clubhouse will be convenient but free from objection. A garage must also be provided.

To best meet all these requirements, a clubhouse located in the center of a course is decidedly bad, while one on the edge has much in its favor.

A few pages back, under the heading of "Good and Bad Shapes," we talked about the location of the clubhouse in direct relation to the course. Better turn back and reread it, as what we said there also applies right here and now.

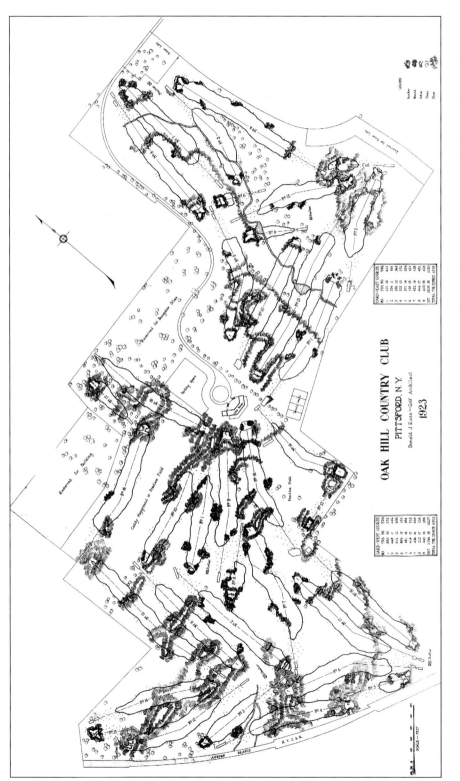

At Oak Hill Country Club in Rochester, NY, a service road stretches well into the property to reach the clubhouse, but doesn't hinder a single hole of the two eighteens.

The Opening Holes

IT IS BEST NOT TO MAKE the first two holes or so too difficult. Give the player a chance to warm up a bit and get
the swing of his stroke well under control. Then give
him some real nuts to crack.

Difficult holes at the start are also apt to cause congestion, holding up the start of the subsequent players,
much to their annoyance.

Location of the first green must ever depend on con-
formation of the land, but all things being equal, a
starting hole in the neighborhood of four hundred
yards is preferable to one shorter.

The out-of-bounds line should be carefully considered in relation to the first hole, so as to avoid the possibility of an opening tee shot being played outside of
the club's property, as is certain to occur when out-of-
bounds runs parallel and close to edge of the first fairway. As a matter of fact, such a thing is undesirable on
any hole. Play up to a boundary line rather than along
it.

It's a beastly nuisance, when starting off play and
before getting limbered up, to drive a ball out-of-
bounds. It generally means delay, loss of a ball, vexa-
tion, and even profanity. Frequently the owners of ad-

The opening hole at Oyster Harbors Golf Club on Cape Cod is long yet inviting, with a single avoidable fairway bunker turning the hole and an ample avenue in front of the green.

jacent property are not very happy about having their grounds invaded and promptly try to make the trespassing players equally unhappy.

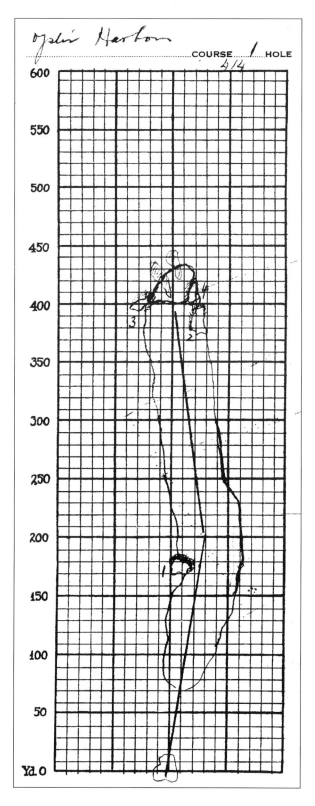

600

550

500

450

400

350

300

250

200

150

100

50

Yd 0

A field sketch of the same first hole at Oyster Harbors. The hole was built to comply with the design.

Zigzag the Holes

DO NOT HAVE THE LINE of fairway always straight from tee to green. Swing it a bit to the right or left. It adds interest by shortening or lengthening the line of play.

Fight shy of all artificial or formal effects. The day of old-fashioned straight edges to the line of fairways is happily past.

Zigzag the holes. Two or three consecutive holes going in the same direction is far from desirable. In fact, it's decidedly monotonous. Having to contend with variable wind conditions adds zest to the game.

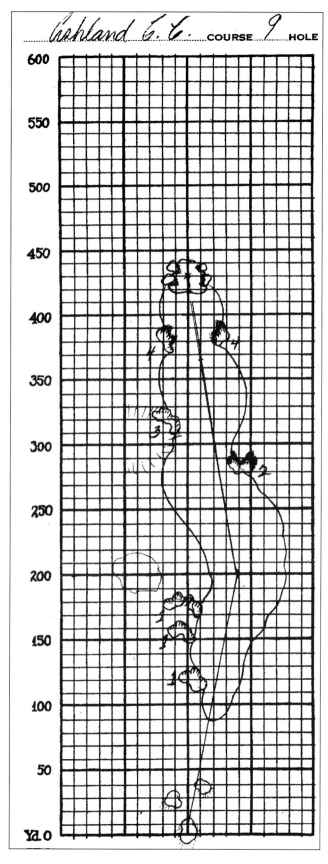

Fairway lines which curve and wrap around hazards look much more natural than straight lines. This is the ninth at Ashland (now Idle Hour Country Club), Lexington, KY.

Where to Put
the Greens

SELECT YOUR PUTTING GREEN LOCATIONS, if possible, to give desirable undulating surfaces. Nature does this sort of thing best. It can be done artificially but must

A simple ridge and swale on a green at Asheville (NC) Country Club (now Grove Park Inn Golf Club) provide plenty of contour to challenge both approach shots and putting.

The bold contours of a Prestwick green could be reproduced in American locations only where moist conditions exist. If dry and hard, such a green is unplayable.

be handled with the highest skill of the golf architect, else disappointment will ever be attendant.

Do not make undulations so severe that the stroke becomes more chance than skill.

Unfortunately, some men in this country have a tendency to take as their models the undulations built on British putting greens, forgetting that climatic conditions are so entirely different over here that they make it well nigh impossible on most courses to keep such undulations in proper putting condition.

Putting greens constructed with relation to the length and topography of the hole are the making of a real golf course.

Your author admits to occasionally ignoring his own advice. This highly undulating, two-level green on the fifth at Scioto Country Club, Columbus, OH was dubbed "ocean waves" by the members.

Modern golf calls for smaller greens. In fact, the art of the mashie niblick has caused entirely new designs for modern greens.

The Best Approach to the Green

A BRITISH PRINCIPLE to be noted is in the placement of the hole in relation to the approach to the green.
Though undulating putting greens have been utilized

Ideal golfing terrain, such as at Ballybunion, consists of knolls and dips that reach right onto the greens to test stance, swing and shot placement.

A slight trench across the seventeenth green at Brae Burn Country Club, West Newton, MA, converts a flat green into a highly intriguing one.

on many American courses, one does not often find what is considered most desirable on a British course, namely an approach which takes the ball over little knolls, undulations and hillocks instead of absolutely flat and smooth country.

There are holes on some Scottish links where knowledge of these peculiarities is absolutely imperative in order to get the ball near the hole. The ball has to be pitched to about a certain spot where it will surely take the roll of the hillocks and stop somewhere near the flag.

Obviously, when such elements govern the approach to the green, the golfing merits of the course are infinitely superior to those on a course where every approach is over a flat surface.

Redan and Punchbowl Greens

A GREEN THAT SLOPES AWAY from the stroke finds little favor because it does not give the player a chance to play as boldly as otherwise. Also, such a green is apt to be more or less blind.

Punchbowl greens are attractive and one or two on a course are much in favor. However, they are not genuine testers of skill, as their sloping sides draw balls toward the center and offer equal advantage to both good and poorly played shots.

Long versus Short Holes

AFTER THE SECOND HOLE you can begin to lay them out with greater license. First and foremost, always strive to take every advantage of natural conditions.

Forget all ideas you may have held as to definite length of certain holes. Make them such length as the property suggests or allows.

After the start off, the holes should increase in difficulty. Try to have one or two short holes in the first nine and two or three in the second nine.

Make all the short holes difficult.

Every course should have at least one long hole. By long, I mean five hundred yards or over. These long holes require much thought to make them attractive. Essentially, they must have natural golfing features, each one making the most of it.

Only when there is a special request for it do I recommend three-shot holes, as the two-shotters are much finer tests of golf.

The number of really fine three-shot holes in this country can be counted on your fingers, while there are hundreds of splendid one- and two-shot holes.

The 194-yard par-3 seventh at Forest Hills Golf Club, Augusta,
GA. Because everyone starts with a level lie of their own choosing
on a par-3, it is not unfair to make par-3s a bit more difficult.

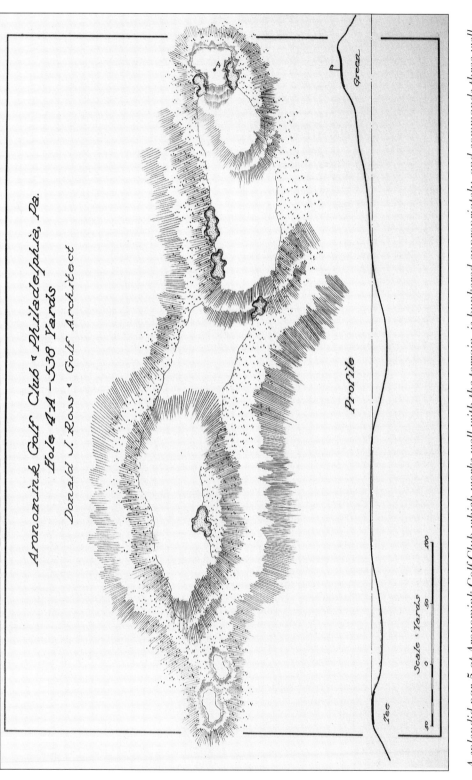

Aronomink Golf Club • Philadelphia, Pa.
Hole 4-A – 538 Yards

Donald J. Ross • Golf Architect

Green

Profile

Tee

Scale • Yards

0   50   100

A splendid par-5 at Aronomink Golf Club which works well with the terrain, is bunkered appropriately; and commands three well-positioned shots.

The dogleg-left tenth at Pine Needles Golf Club in North Carolina. Two bunkers at the turn force many to aim right, and thus make a longer hole of it.

A dogleg hole is really one of the most delightful type on any course. It affords pleasure to all classes of players. It is an easy matter to bunker it successfully.

Adjustable Tees

ANOTHER PROPOSITION that we are now taking advantage of is the adjustable tee. This means having two or more tees for every hole, each more than twenty yards long.

With long tees, it is possible to adjust the markers according to the prevailing wind. The greenkeeper can move them up on windy days and on days when the turf is soft and the ball does not get its proper roll. When the wind does not menace, when the course is baked hard so that brassie and good iron shots are more possible for distance, when the tee shot can produce thirty yards more of distance with the bound and roll of the ball, then the tee must be moved back.

This idea makes the hole present the same possiblities each period of the season, and is one of the most important ones to consider in building a course.

The old courses in England had separate tees at every hole. The old courses had tees so long and wide that you never knew what kind of shot you were going to have at any given hole.

A hole that is a drive and a mashie on one day, may be two full woods the next. No matter where a player may be in the habit of driving, he may have an entirely different second shot to play each day. One day, under

Your author was the first to advocate and routinely construct two or more tee boxes per hole. Shown here: the sixth at Scioto.

some conditions, a pitch may be the shot. Some other time from the same spot, a low run-up will be the only effective stroke.

The modern golf course should either have tees fifty yards long or three or four separate tees at every hole.

Tees that point from various angles to the green also give a chance to take care of conditions.

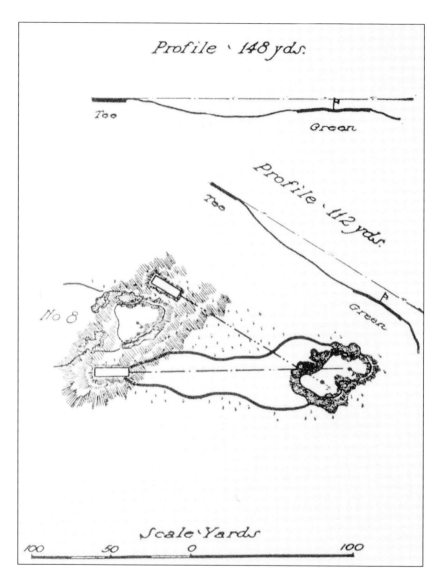

Two separate tees at different angles, combined with a long diagonal green, effectively create two separate par-3s for the ninth at Gulf Stream Golf Club, Delray Beach, FL.

Your author hitting to one of his prettiest water holes, the par-3 third at Pine Needles Golf Club, Southern Pines, NC.

Water Hazards

WATER HAZARDS ALWAYS LEND welcome variety and test of skill to a course. They are pleasant breaks that can generally be made into charming beauty spots.

But don't allow your enthusiasm for them to run away with your good judgment. Limit the number of water hazards to three. Two might be better. The repeated loss of balls by those to whom the hazard is difficult is apt to create dissatisfaction.

Should your property happily have a brook running through it, choice treatments can be secured by arranging one hole parallel with it and another so the drive or second shot must cross it.

If there happens to be a swamp on your ground, it might offer an opportunity to build a putting green by filling it in and raising the green to a higher level.

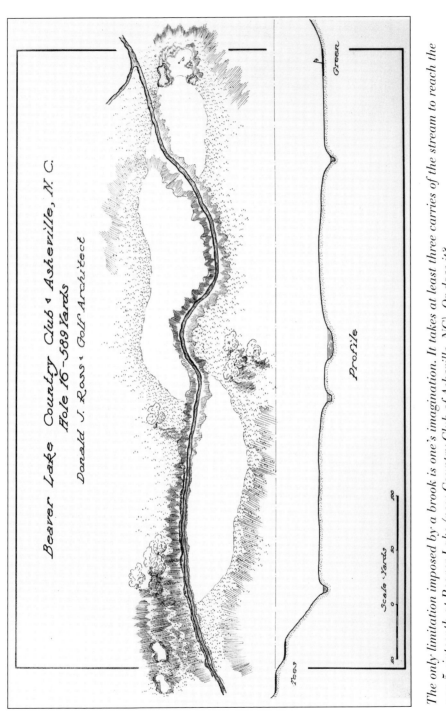

The only limitation imposed by a brook is one's imagination. It takes at least three carries of the stream to reach the par-5 sixteenth at Beaver Lake (now Country Club of Asheville, NC). Or does it?

Blind Shots

On two-shot holes it is highly desirable in many cases to compel the player to place his tee shot so that his shot to the green may be clear, and if not properly placed, the shot to the green may to some extent be blind.

The shot is slightly downhill on the par-3 twelfth at Kernwood Country Club, Salem, MA, but the green is canted to greet the flight of the ball.

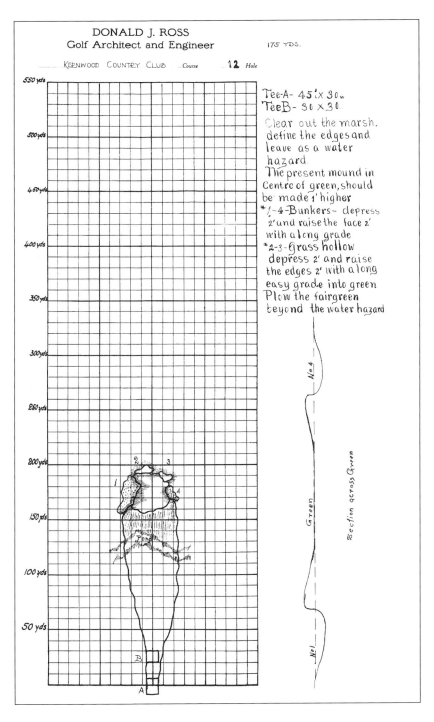

DONALD J. ROSS
Golf Architect and Engineer   175 YDS.

KERNWOOD COUNTRY CLUB   Course   12 Hole

Tee-A- 45ᴸx 30ᵂ
TeeB- 30 X 30

Clear out the marsh.
define the edges and
leave as a water
hazard.
The present mound in
Centre of green, should
be made 1' higher
*1-4-Bunkers- depress
2' and raise the face 2'
with a long grade
*2-3-Grass hollow
depress 2' and raise
the edges 2' with a long
easy grade into green
Plow the fairgreen
beyond the water hazard

A diagram of the same hole, complete with construction instructions and a cross-section of the dish-shaped green.

On undulating land, blind shots are bound to occur, and one or two of them are not at all serious. Truth be told, I rather like them, as they add a bit of spice to the game.

But I'll offer an argument against a blind green: Suppose a player having the honor (or who is playing the odd) should lay his ball stiff to the pin. Think how much harder it becomes for the opponent to follow suit when the ball is in view, the ball seeming to act as an added hazard. Such a mental condition would hardly exist if the ball was not clearly in sight. And it seems only fair that a player making such a shot should be entitled to all fair advantage.

For short holes, I lean toward placing the green above the tee level, one that meets the ball. But such a green should never be blind.

The putting green should be in full view on all short holes.

Long and Short Par 4s

THE DRIVE-AND-LONG-APPROACH HOLE is a pleasing length and must have its place on every first-class layout. By this I mean one that demands a long second to the green, a hole, say, from four hundred twenty-five to four hundred fifty yards, according to the lay of the land and wind conditions. I favor at least two holes of this length in each nine.

We must also provide at least one or two drive-and-pitch-length holes. Such holes are delightful if properly constructed, but decidedly the reverse otherwise.

In holes of this length, both the drive and approach should be difficult. Otherwise, they are usually very uninteresting.

Every hole should have a number of tees, particularly the drive-and-long-approach ones, so that under all weather conditions the hole may retain its proper playing length.

Tees should be located as near to putting greens as possible without endangering players. Long walks to tees cause much dissatisfaction.

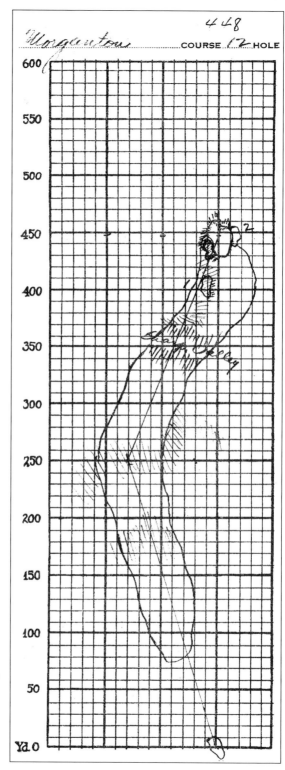

The twelfth at Mimosa Hills Golf Club, Morganton, NC, is a strong par-4. To reach the green in regulation, one must carry the bunkers short of the green.

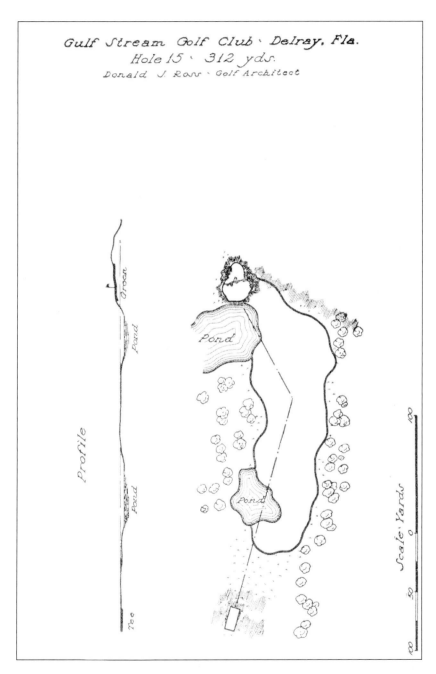

Gulf Stream Golf Club · Delray, Fla.
Hole 15 · 312 yds.
Donald J. Ross · Golf Architect

Profile

Green

Pond

Pond

Pond

Pond

Scale Yards

A short par 4 where the drive must be precisely positioned in order to minimize the difficulty of the second shot.

Many Long Courses are Uninteresting

THE DESIRABLE LENGTH for a good course is from 6,000 to 6,400 yards.

But bear in mind that it is quality, not quantity, that counts.

In my work I repeatedly have had trouble making committees see the force of this. They seem possessed with the idea that length is the main desideratum. It is beyond all argument that many a long course is noticeably uninteresting, in contrast to shorter ones that are well thought-out and skillfully constructed.

Seventy per cent of the courses in Great Britain are under 6,000 yards, and some of the finest links in the world are over there. In this country, there seems to have been a desire for length. The result is that we see layouts 6,500 yards long, and some of them will not begin to compare with courses a thousand yards shorter.

Just as fine a round of golf can be had on a short course as can be had on one of 6,500 yards.

The tendency today in golf course architecture is toward tightening the holes rather than in excessive length.

There should be two ways to play a hole, one for a physically strong, and one for the man not so strong. The holes should be trapped so that par golf depends upon skill rather than upon physical strength.

Nine versus Eighteen Holes

BETTER A CHOICE NINE-HOLE COURSE than an indifferent eighteen-hole one.

Some tracts are admirable for nine holes, but make abominable eighteen-hole courses.

Strange to say, some committees seem determined that they shall have an eighteen-hole course, irrespective of whether there is sufficient area.

It very frequently occurs that a club is well able to keep a nine-hole course in fine shape but cannot conveniently carry the load of an eighteen-hole one.

This is a point that should carry much weight. Nothing is quite as disastrous to the popularity and prosperity of a club as an unkempt course.

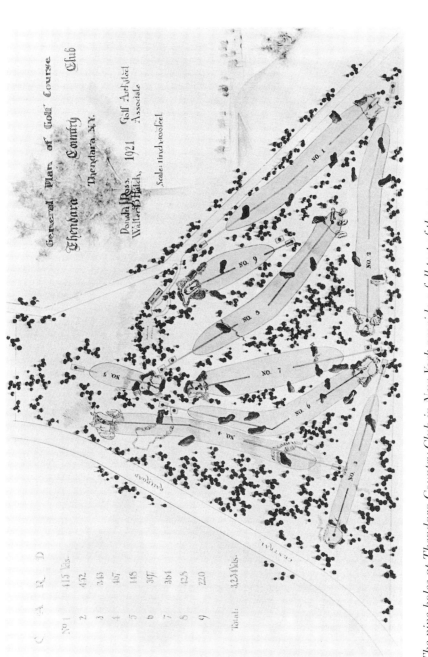

The nine holes at Thendara Country Club in New York provide a full test of the game.

Bunkers

A GOLF COURSE WITHOUT BUNKERS is a very monotonous affair. Yet I have seen courses with numbers of them so badly placed that they were practically useless.

Bunkers should be so placed as to be clearly in view, and in such locations as to make all classes of players think.

Often, the very highest recommendation of a bunker is when it is criticized. That shows that it is accomplishing the one thing for which it was built: It is making players think.

How often do we hear players criticize a bunker that is placed for a carry as being an unfair one if they cannot carry it?

But don't misunderstand me, and think I advocate the placement of bunkers so they will always compel players to play short or off the direct line to the hole, although I do think that occasionally this can be done with perfect license.

Provided there is ample acreage for the proper layout of a course, it is a very simple matter to furnish a line of play on every hole that can be taken without ever having to negotiate bunker carries, but at the same time will force the player to sacrifice one or more strokes, should he choose to take the easy way.

Then again, sometimes it is desirable to provide a carry which compels a player to either take it or play short.

Our aim is a variety of bunkering that will multiply the interest of the game. So, logically, the placement of bunkers must be left to the skill and ingenuity of the golf architect.

Inasmuch as the greatest number of members in every club play for pleasure, the expert must avoid going to extremes, keep that class of player always in mind, and do as much as he can to help him keep up pleasure and enjoyment in the game.

I have evidence in my work at Pinehurst, North Carolina, that a course bunkered fairly and scientifically is the most attractive. During the construction and bunkering of the Number Two Course, a large number of our very best golfing friends complained bitterly about what seemed to them very radical steps that we were taking. They predicted that it would be a course very little used.

At the time, our Number One Course was rather easy and quite free from bunkers, and was not comparable in difficulty or as a test of golf.

Before Number Two was open many days, we were confronted with the problem of what regulations we could make to relieve the congestion resulting from the desertion of Number One. This difficulty has been confronting us ever since. Those men who were so skeptical are now Number Two's strongest admirers.

Bunkers on the thirteenth at Salem Country Club in Massachusetts transform a routine par-4 into one that commands attention.

No Bunker Is Misplaced

THERE IS NO SUCH THING as a misplaced bunker.

Regardless of where a bunker may be, it is the business of the player to avoid it.

The par-3 fifth at Interlachen near Minneapolis is the most heavily bunkered hole on the course. The way to avoid them is to hit the green.

Scooped-Out Pits

TO PROVIDE THIS TYPE OF BUNKER, you must have undulating ground, as they can only be constructed on the faces of slopes or knolls.

I like them very much, as they usually have a natural appearance and are nearly always open to view, a desirable thing in all bunkers.

To keep them in condition, sand must be used plentifully. The whole scooped-out surface should be completely covered with it.

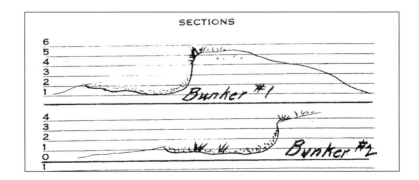

Cross-section of scooped-out pits.

To make it visible from the tee, the sand was swept to the top of the pit on this fairway bunker at the eighteenth at Oakland Hills. But note the ribbon of turf on the greenside pit between the sand and the top edge.

The designs for such bunkers are rather flexible, allowing you to make some wide and shallow, and others narrow and deep.

The short par-3 third at Wannamoisett Country Club, Rumford, RI, shows that a scooped-out pit can sometimes be massive.

A ribbon of turf can stabilize the steep face of a scooped-out pit, as here on the eleventh at Beverly Country Club in Chicago.

Sunken Pits with Raised Faces

A HAZARD OF THIS KIND is usually built on flat ground and is particularly serviceable on clay land, where digging is so expensive and drainage so uncertain.

By cutting a sunken pit out one-and-a-half-feet deep, the face can be raised a like amount using the fill,

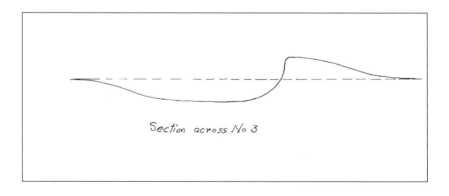

Section across No 3

Cross-section of a sunken pit with raised face.

Without the raised faces, the bunkers on the old eighth at Inverness in Toledo are hardly hazards.

giving a finished face of three feet. (This depth is arbitrary, and I simply use it by way of example.)

If the raised part is carefully designed and built, it can be made to appear quite natural. If you use a line and square in the building of this variety of bunker, the result is sure to have an artificialness akin to the hideous. It's just as easy to break up all the lines and avoid such a regrettable result.

Raised faces should be asymmetrical. The farther off line a shot is in any bunker on the fifth at Brae Burn Country Club, West Newton, MA, the higher the bank over which one must play.

Pot Bunkers

SUCH BUNKERS ARE TOTALLY below the surface. They are most generally placed in the neighborhood of the green.

Particular attention should be paid when locating them to secure good drainage.

These pot bunkers at the ninth at Longmeadow Country Club, Springfield, MA, have sand pulled to the top.

But these pot bunkers on the eighteenth at Worcester (MA) Country Club are virtually flat, with grass faces.

Your author even used pot bunkers successfully as fairway hazards, as on the ninth at Miami Valley Country Club in Dayton,. OH.

The tenth at Dayton (OH) Country Club. If not overdone, a pot bunker is very effective on a drive-and-pitch hole.

Mound and Pot Combinations

WHERE IT IS DESIRABLE to cover a large area of ground, hazards of this kind can be used advantageously. A mound and pot bunker combination is particularly helpful in dividing the line of play on parallel holes, it being equally hazardous for both holes.

The pits in such a combination may be shallow and the mounds should be covered with coarse grass. But it is not necessary to fill these shallow pits with any sand. Both high parts and hollows may be covered over with coarse grass if desired.

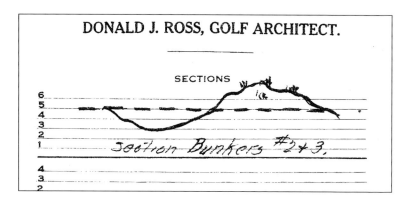

Cross-section of a bunker and mound combination.

*A bunker & mound combination edges the fairway on the par-4
sixteenth at Siwanoy Country Club, Bronxville, NY.*

Diagonal Bunkers

HERE IS A GOOD HAZARD that I feel to be a very fair one. It can be built for either a tee shot or a second shot, providing a carry of any desired length. It affords a fair test for any length of shot. If placed properly, the longer the carry taken, the greater the advantage gained.

It is a noticeable trait that most American courses are deficient in the delightful feature of long carries. Diagonal bunkers are a splendid type to use in providing long carries.

Diagonal hazards on the green approach at Interlachen's twelfth.

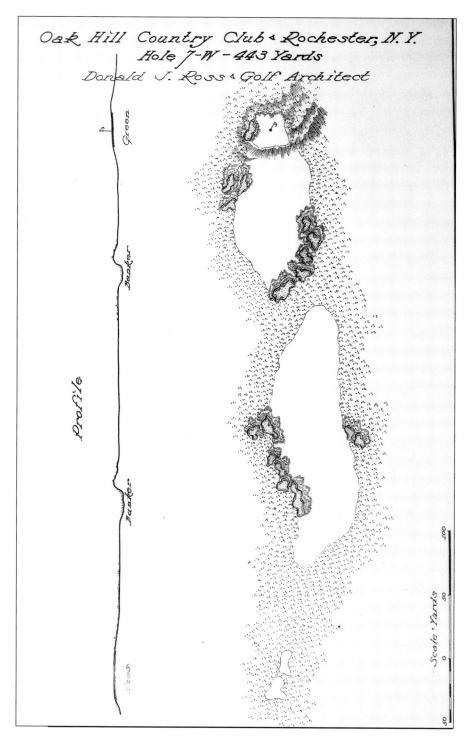

Oak Hill Country Club ◦ Rochester, N.Y.
Hole 7-W - 443 Yards
Donald J. Ross ◦ Golf Architect

Profile

Green

Bunker

Bunker

Tees

Scale Yards

0   50   100

Diagonal hazards test both the drive and second shots on the par-4 seventh of the West Course at Oak Hill Country Club in Rochester, NY.

Natural Hazards

By NATURAL HAZARDS, we refer to ravines, broken faces of the land, brooks, and the like, each of which should be used to its best advantage.

There is something so undeniably pleasant about a natural hazard that it seems out of the question to duplicate it artificially. Take, for instance, a creek found on a property. Something about the way the banks have shaped themselves adds greatly to their attractiveness. But when a like effect is attempted artificially, it falls far short, no matter what pains and expense are taken. Man cannot do in a few days what nature took years to accomplish.

Should you be so fortunate as to have a creek running through your property, a very interesting treatment is that of having it run across the line of play on some hole and parallel with the line of another.

Don't, however, make the creek the only hazard, as is frequently done by running holes parallel to it just for the sake of getting the creek on all possible holes. Avoid such a monotony. Variety is the spice of golf, just as it is of life.

In any event, too many water hazards are not desirable, as the loss of balls becomes a serious detraction from the joys of the game.

One of the most natural of golf holes, the fifth (now seventh) at Toledo's Inverness Club rises from creek valley to hilltop green, with nary a bunker.

In this connection, I recall an amusing incident on a New Jersey course where a club member, in very poor form that day, drove six successive balls into a little pond. He was so totally disgusted with both himself and the game that in desperation he pitched his clubs in also, and did not come to the course again for six weeks—a week for each ball lost. An accurate record of his profanity, happily, was not preserved.

Hummocks

ANYONE WHO HAS BEEN PRIVILEGED to play such courses as Prestwick, St. Andrews, Dornoch or North Berwick in Scotland cannot forget the joys of those tantalizing little hummocks and the golfing appearance they give to those courses. Over and over again, my American friends who have played those British courses remark to me on the charming variation one gets in the lies on fairways and the shots up to the hole where hummocks exist.

They certainly do provide a test in playing the ball from all kinds of stances.

If, by any chance, hummocks are to be found on your property, by all means make the most of them. To some extent, it is also possible to make them artificially.

Where not desirable to penalize a shot with a pit, particularly in the vicinity of the green, artificial hummocks can be built, giving the player who is off line a more difficult shot than the one who has played straight.

It is sometimes even advisable to put such hummocks directly in front of a green. They add interest to the playing of the shot up to the hole. Nothing is quite so good for testing approach shots.

Artificial hummocks frame the putting surface on the short par-4 second at Brae Burn Country Club.

Hummocks of sand on the ninth and elsewhere at Rhode Island Country Club have been called 'inverted bunkers' by members.

Irregular Mounds

WHEN ROCKS ARE PLENTIFUL and have to be removed,
they can be used in building mounds.

Fight shy of building them on regular lines. Follow
nature as far as possible.

Vary them in size, according to location.

They may be used in the same way as the mound
and pit combination in the dividing of parallel fairways.

They are not, however, always desirable in front of
greens, particularly if they prove to be so high as to
make the shot blind.

Irregular mounds at Interlachen are useful in separating parallel fairways.

Often called 'chocolate drops,' the irregular mounds to the left of the first green at Essex County Club, Manchester, MA, are as effective a hazard as a bunker.

Long Grass

IN THE BRITISH COURSES, heather, whins, and bent grass are in many cases left growing in a diagonal formation, producing a remarkably interesting hazard. The best we can do over here is to let our grass grow long, following somewhat the same formation.

As a savings in mowing expense and as a hazard, long grass can be left in front of every tee, varying in width from seventy to one hundred twenty yards. On short holes of one hundred fifty yards or less, it ought not to be necessary to cut any of the grass, except at intervals to keep it at such a height that balls will not continually be lost.

Such grass can also be left in patches through the fairway, where it will be of good service in stopping the run of topped balls.

Grass Hollows

ANOTHER PARTICULARLY JOYFUL MEMORY of Scottish courses are the grass hollows that jut into the greens here and there, giving the putting green a charming irregularity, posing to the player something to think about, and making him use care in handling recovery strokes.

Artificial hollows are only practical in this country on slopes where natural drainage conditions are good. Otherwise, the water is unduly held, making the grass grow coarse and rank, a rather undesirable condition, particularly if the hollow is part of the putting green.

It is also well to bear in mind that the water lying in such hollows during the winter causes winter-kill, necessitating returfing or resowing each spring.

When a green is situated in a punchbowl, it is often very helpful to build grass hollows on the sloping sides to catch the flow of heavy rain water and dispose of it in a way that prevents harm to the green.

They can also be used to advantage on the sides of fairways for hooked or sliced balls. When so placed, they should always have good drainage.

Another thing in their favor is the ease with which they can be kept in condition.

Where favorable conditions exist, grass hollows should be plentiful on a course.

This punchbowl green is doomed to failure. Water will pour off the steep slopes and onto the putting surface, filling it, like a punchbowl.

A more sensible punchbowl effect was achieved with a grass hollow behind the tenth green at Inverness, which captures water off the back hillside.

So deep was the ravine on the twelfth at the Country Club of Buffalo, that the bottom turned into an attractive pond.

Deep Grass Ravines

DEEP GRASS RAVINES are truly a delightful type of hazard.

To say here how they can be utilized is, however, out of the question, as the topography of each property must designate their treatment.

But they make a very lovely hazard, and I lose no opportunity to use them in every possible way.

I am reminded of my friend Alec Campbell, who is noted for his frank, pithy way of making observations. One day he was asked by an enthusiastic club member what he thought of a certain course, to which he answered, "Not very much." Not satisfied, still another question was plied, concerning what should be done to make it a good course. "Well," said my friend Alec, "it would require a damned earthquake.

"And plenty of topdressing."

Building the Course

Now that we have agreed upon the location, length and general treatment of the holes, greens and hazards, we must start construction of the course based on a carefully thought-out plan.

If the soil is a sandy loam, construction problems will be decidedly less than with clay soils. Brush, trees and rocks can more readily be removed, bunkers more easily dug and greens more easily built. Drainage problems are reduced to a minimum.

Frequently, courses are on both sandy loam and clay, so let's first talk over the general land preparation that applies, no matter what the soil. Then we can go into the specific handling of greens under differing conditions.

Clearing the land is naturally the first consideration. So we will start by removing any boulders.

Your author saw all manner of construction equipment in the course of his career, from horse and slip scrapers to tractors . . .

. . . to steamshovels to bulldozers.

Boulders

THE USUAL-SIZED STONES or boulders will be but little
bother to remove.

For the larger ones, up to even four tons, I have had
splendid results using a Connecticut Rock Puller, which
lifts boulders bodily out of the ground, with only two

Many a fairway starts in this condition.

It takes enormous manpower to clear land of rocks and boulders and make it playable for golf.

men required to operate it. A strong point in favor of this machine is that it can be used to carry boulders to any spot desired, saving much time and labor cost.

If it is not necessary to actually remove smaller boulders, an easy and effectual way to get them out of the way is to dig around and underneath them, topple them over into a hole deep enough to bed them at least a foot below the surface, and then cover them with soil. In cases where the fill material needed for large boulder holes is scarce, this method of disposal of even large boulders is most convenient and economical.

When ledge rock or large surface rock appears, its location dictates whether it is best to blast it out or cover it up. If it interferes with the line of play, you must blast it out to at least two feet below the surface. Before covering over with topsoil, it is desirable to cover it with from three to six inches of clay to prevent the rock from drawing moisture out of the soil. If you fail to do this, you are bound to have a burnt patch during hot summer months.

Should a surface ledge rock not interfere with the line of play, cover it with clay and soil and utilize it as a flat hummock.

If rocks high out of the ground are fortunately located, they can be left right where they are, smaller ones pulled around it, and the whole mass covered with clay and soil so it can be used as a mound.

Stone walls that may be on the property are admirable for the same purpose, but frequently it is possible to sell the rocks in such walls, which is quite the happiest happening.

Making the most of existing rock conditions not only goes a long way toward making the course one of interest, but also greatly lessens the construction expense, a point always to be considered.

If rocks in swampy land have to be removed, I have had better success using oxen instead of horses, it being almost impossible to get horses to do such work satisfactorily. Oxen are more patient. To do it by hand is very expensive.

Speaking about expense, I recall an instance where it costs $2,000 to haul off rocks from a course. Instead of hauling those rocks away, it would have been just as well to have used them in building mounds, saving much bunkering expense. This needless expenditure was pointed out by this expert when sought for advice.

Trees

As beautiful as trees are, and as fond as you and I are of them, we still must not lose sight of the fact that there is a limited place for them in golf. We must not allow our sentiments to crowd out the real intent of a golf course, that of providing fair playing conditions. If it in any way interferes with a properly played stroke, I think the tree is an unfair hazard and should not be allowed to stand.

On the other hand, there is no need to ruthlessly cut down everything before us. If it can be arranged so that holes are slightly elbowed, trees can frequently be spared. On hot summer days they are most welcome, especially around tee boxes.

In Scotland and England they have their heather, broom and whins to lend delightful color and variety to the courses. So we must go about this tree matter carefully over here, else we will have a barren, devastated appearance on many of our courses.

In felling a tree of less than six inches in diameter at the stump, cut off the head to within two feet of the bottom and drag it out by the roots with a Hercules or some equally good stump puller.

When a tree is larger than six inches in diameter, dig around the roots and cut off all the main ones, then

Two views of the seventeenth at Biltmore Forest Country Club, Asheville, NC, showing (top) clearing of trees between tee and fairway, and (bottom) finished product with accents of trees but no intrusions.

fasten a rope to the head of the tree well up toward the top. Half a dozen men can then pull it over. The tremendous leverage to which the tree lends itself will result in its own destruction.

For a still larger tree, it is best to cut it down to within two feet of the bottom and blast the stump into parts, then use the stump puller to drag out the pieces. One charge of dynamite will generally do the work.

This last method is very satisfactory as it tears out practically all bothersome roots, overcoming the necessity of digging them out.

Brush

CUT OUT ALL BRUSH, pile it in heaps and burn. If roots are too large for a plough to tear out, then grub the larger ones, removing them completely.

Now that we have the rocks, trees, and brush taken care of, next comes drainage.

Don't Slight Drainage

WHATEVER YOU DON'T DO, don't slight drainage. It is of first importance and should be given much thought. Many an otherwise highly satisfactory course has been a constant disappointment either because drainage problems were not properly handled or parsimony of the club prevented it from being done.

Drainage is essential to secure proper playing conditions under varying weather conditions. Otherwise, after a rainstorm, or even a shower, you must wait for hours, if not days, for the course to again become satisfactorily playable. It is a well-known fact that badly drained land will positively not produce satisfactory turf for golfing purposes.

In soils with subsoils of gravel or sand, drainage is natural. Such may be the case on certain parts of your tract, but don't take it for granted that it is generally across the property. Make sure as you go along.

With heavy clay soils that show evidence of sourness, money must be spent for their drainage. Just how this drainage can best be accomplished is unquestionably work for an expert. Don't start by trying to save the cost of such expert advice, for you most assuredly won't save it in the end.

No definite rules can be laid down as to what size tile

pipe should be employed or what depth to dig the drains. Only the specific conditions on each property can determine its treatment.

However, on average land it would be safe to say that the main drain ought to be from three to three-and-one-half feet deep, and six-inch tile used. For lateral drains leading into it, use the same depth and four-inch tiles.

Before covering the tile up, be sure to cover the upper half of the joints with good quality tar paper to help prevent sand or loose filling from washing into the tile. You can help secure good drainage by filling the ditch to within a foot of the top with good clean gravel or cinders, and then put on topsoil.

In swampy places where there is very little foundation to support pipe, planks should be placed end to end the length of the ditch and the tile laid on them. This will keep them from sinking, which causes the joints to open and fill, defeating the very purpose of the drain.

Satisfactory results can often be secured in swampy land by using stone drains. In this case, the ditch should then be cut much wider. Then, selecting even-sized stones, lay them along the sides of the bottom and cover them with flat stones. On top of them put small-size rocks, and on top of them still smaller, and so on, finishing up with gravel and topsoil.

Drainage, Drainage, Drainage

GET THIS FACT FIRMLY IN YOUR MIND. Drainage—careful, thorough drainage—is the vital element to success in any putting green.

This being so, it's surprising how it is so often neglected during the construction of a large number of present-day courses.

It is absolutely impossible to produce a healthy growth of dwarf grasses on imperfectly drained soil. It must ever mean problems that the greenkeeper will never overcome, save by ripping up the entire putting green and doing it as it should have been done in the first place.

Time and time again, when called to visit courses in an advisory way, I have been confronted with the question, "What can be the matter with our greens?" Upon examination, in nine cases out of ten, the poor conditions have proved to be due to wrong or insufficient drainage.

If rightly attended to in the first place, during the construction of the greens, much future expense can be spared, to say nothing of the nerve-wracking difficulties that must inevitably confront the green committee.

Draining Putting Greens on Sandy Loam

WITH SANDY LOAM that has a gravel subsoil, putting green construction is not difficult. All they usually need are compost and humus dug well in, to give the necessary percolation conditions for surface drainage.

Drainage problems concern chiefly the clay soils, and they are indeed difficult.

Draining Putting Greens on Clay Soils

First, perhaps we'd better talk over the best method, the one that, although costly, is far and away the most desirable.

Remove from entire size of the green, both topsoil and subsoil, to a depth of eighteen inches, being careful not to needlessly mix the two soils. On this cleared foundation open a main drain, a foot deep through the center of the green. It should be dug V-shaped, at least two feet across the top. Lead this drain to a convenient outlet. If there is no such outlet, then carry it to a dry well six feet deep by five feet across, dug a little ways from the green. Fill this hole with good-sized stones. This well will usually care for all surplus water from any good-sized green.

Leading to the center drain, dig V-shaped laterals, each a foot deep and two feet wide at the top. Two or three on each side are generally enough. The center drain should have six-inch tile, and the laterals three-inch tile. Cover the upper half of all the joints with tar paper and fill the ditches with coarse gravel or good clean cinders.

Now, over the entire cleaned foundation of the green, spread a three- or four-inch layer of coarse gravel or clean cinders. Follow with four inches of subsoil, mixed thoroughly with coarse sand. Then comes your topsoil, well-mixed with coarse sand and pulverized charcoal. Now add the desired undulations. Cover the whole surface with a good dressing of lime, and harrow it well into the surface.

After two weeks or so, the lime will have counteracted the acidity found in almost all heavy clay soils. Next, cover the entire green with a heavy dressing of humus or well-rotted stable manure. Fork this into the soil not more than three or four inches deep. This treatment permits surplus water to percolate to the water table of cinders below and be carried away by the drain pipes, forming a continually healthy home for grass roots. The cinders also hold a certain amount of the moisture, supplying it to the roots when most required.

If the soil is not treated in this manner, in the summer it becomes hard on the surface. Then, whenever rains fall, the water simply washes away, none of it being stored in the soil for future use.

A Cheaper Method of Draining Putting Greens

LIKE MOST THINGS THAT STOP SHORT of being the best, this less-costly method is not as good, but in some cases it is nevertheless used, and is far and away better than nothing.

First, dig the main drain through the center and then open up the laterals leading to it, all of them being two-and-one-half feet deep. Six-inch tile should be laid in the main drain, and three-inch in the laterals. Lead the main drain to some convenient outlet or a dry well as described in the preceding method. Cover the upper half of all joints of the tiles with tar paper, and fill the ditches with a foot of coarse gravel or clean cinders, on top of which replace the topsoil.

Now lay on a heavy dressing of coarse sand and spade up the whole green a foot deep, thoroughly mixing in the sand. Be careful to remove all roots and stones. Everything is now ready to form the desired undulations.

After this has been done, topdress the entire green with pulverized charcoal and lime, harrowing or raking it well into the soil. After two or more weeks the lime will have sweetened the soil, making it ready for a heavy topdressing of humus or well-rotted manure. Under no conditions apply the lime and manure at the same time.

Drain tiles are essential to a green, regardless of the drainage method utilized.

Don't Build Greens and Mounds Separately

WHEN WORKING IN A FLAT AREA, I intentionally build up the greens and surround them with mounds, as that is the only way they can be built to stand out distinctly on low, flat land.

I think the best way to get the contours of both the green and mounds to blend without any artifical appearance is to start the fills in the following manner:

Stake the outer edge of the green very carefully and, at close intervals, set grade stakes to conform to the fills shown on the sketches. Do the same with the mounds.

Then dump the fill, which should be largely sand or fine gravel, roughly up to the finished grade.

The next step is to disc harrow the whole area, green and mounds, into one rolling mass.

After discing, float carefully so as to work out all hollows and sharp edges. Then smooth by hand, raking

Stages of green construction. First, topsoil is removed to install drain tile.

the putting surface particularly so that it will conform very nearly to the finished grades.

Then cover the green with eight inches of good heavy soil to which has been added local peat and a small quantity of sand.

Finish the surface with four inches of screened topsoil to which has been added a quantity of peat and coarse sand.

The mounds should be covered with eight inches of soil, to which may be added some peat.

If you attempt to build the greens and mounds separately, you are sure to get an artificial appearance.

After topsoil is replaced, it is floated out into appropriate contours (right team) and bunkers shaped (left team).

The finished green flows seamlessly into the surrounding landscape.

When to Prepare Putting Greens

THE PREPARATION OF PUTTING GREENS should always be done considerably in advance of seeding, to allow ample time for the sinking of soil and the smoothing over above the drains, which are bound to sink a certain amount. If it is intended to sow greens in the fall, it is best to construct them in the early summer.

Building Tees

ALL THROUGH LIFE we are continually running up against people who are ever striving to reduce things to measurements. They seem unable to grasp quality, so they must ever judge things by a scale of measurements.

Nearly every committee has at least one such man, who insists on the tape measure method of doing things. If such a chap is apt to dominate a committee, the result is a course of deadly monotony. For instance, he'll insist that every tee should be a certain size, irrespective of location or governing conditions.

There are two, and only two, inflexible rules for laying out a tee: It should be big, and the top must be perfectly level.

How pleasing is the impression we get of a course when the tee is in the pink of condition. What a delightful intimation it is of the joys the course has in store for us.

This being so, isn't it strange that, as a rule, the upkeep of tees in this country is so indifferently considered?

In locating your tees, a naturally level site is of course preferable, but it is sometimes necessary to build the tee up so the view of the landing place of the ball or the green will be clearly in sight. When such is the case, by all means do not make the terraces abrupt. Give them long slopes. It is less artificial in its effect and lessens the effort of reaching them.

In making elevated tees, let me again put the loud pedal on their size. Make them big enough so that the player will have a breadth of feeling, and not feel as if precariously placed on top of a packing box, where any unguarded move endangers his falling off.

Another thing against a small tee is that it does not offer enough room to shift the markers from day to day, to distribute wear and tear. In such situations, it is out of the question to expect your greenkeeper to have the tees in good condition.

Don't let your domineering tape-measure man insist it is essential that the tee be cut square to the line of

A typical tee box at Essex County Club, with plenty of flexibility and gentle slopes.

Precarious is not the only term that fits this tee box. Preposterous also comes to mind.

play. Frequently there are locations where a diagonal tee is good, especially when it allows movement of the markers to give variation in the length of the hole.

Draining Tees

DRAINAGE OF TEES is not as important as for putting greens, so it is not necessary to go to the same expense. Nevertheless, it is essential to provide good open soil so that grasses generally sown for tee purposes will flourish freely.

When the soil is a sandy loam with sand or gravel subsoil, a light digging and a supply of necessary plant food is all that is required. In case of clay soil, dig it over a foot deep and mix thoroughly with coarse sand. The surface should then be liberally supplied with plant food in the form of humus or compost.

Let me caution you that we must not depend too much upon commercial fertilizers for development of tees or grasses. They are valuable as a stimulant to boost the grass along, but they contribute very few lasting benefits to the soil.

Do you see what great importance it is that the mechanical condition and content of the soil shall be in the right shape before sowing of any seed? A soil having an open texture and long enduring fertility is the ideal one.

Preparing Fairways

On SHORT HOLES, the land should be cleared about thirty yards wide. If there is dense growth on the sides, make it considerably wider, and overcome that most annoying aspect of short holes, the continual loss of balls.

On long holes, the clearing should be from sixty to ninety yards in width, governed by the length of the hole.

Right here, let me put in another plea against the tape-measure man who insists on the width from tee to hole being the same throughout. For my part, a hole that has a fairway more or less irregular in lines is decidedly more pleasurable to play, especially if allowed to irregularly narrow up toward the tee and green.

After all clearing is done, plough the areas intended to be fairways.

In case of clay lands, particular attention must be given to those parts most generally in play, which is to say, where tee shots land, as well as all approaches to greens.

Thoroughly pulverize the soil by disk-harrowing in different directions. If coarse sand is available, give these parts a good heavy dressing and work in with tooth harrows. See that all holes from stump or rock removal are filled and in good shape.

It may be necessary to drag-harrow parts of the fairway to smooth it over.

Not long ago I was asked to visit a prominent course to advise, among other things, what should be done to put a large portion of the fairways into proper playing condition. I found that all the trouble was caused by neglect of those who built the course to properly level the surface from which stumps and rocks had been cleared.

All the fairways were broken into sharp little hollows and the only remedy was to take up the turf, fill those hollows and re-lay the turf again. Of course, this entailed an enormous expense that could very easily have been avoided when the land was originally being prepared for seeding.

In the construction of present-day courses, a good deal more attention is being given to fairway preparation during construction than formerly. That is a good thing.

Ploughing

IF THE TRACT IS COVERED with fairly good quality turf, ploughing is not necessary from the tee ahead to a hundred yards off the tee. This part can generally be put in playable condition by topdressing and seeding. It is not really important to give this portion of the course much attention, as perfection here is not desirable. All other parts of the fairway should be ploughed a good depth, but not so deep as to turn over the subsoil. It should be apparent that the thinner the topsoil, the shallower the ploughing should be.

On clay soils, deep ploughing is of greater importance, as it helps open it up and permits better drainage. Pulverizing such soils is the desirable thing. Deep ploughing helps to accomplish it.

Lay on the Lime

LIMING IS THE NEXT OPERATION.

It is a recognized fact that a majority of clay lands are deficient in lime, and contain a good deal of acidity detrimental to the healthy development of grass. To overcome this, it is generally advisable to follow up after the disc-harrowing with a dressing of lime over all the ploughed parts. About a ton or more to the acre is the usual quantity required. Tooth-harrowing will thoroughly incorporate the lime with the soil.

There are several satisfactory machines on the market for the even distribution of lime, which not only spread evenly but are a distinct saving in time and labor costs.

After the lime has done its part, say in about two weeks, treat all parts (except from the tee to a hundred yards off the front of the tee) with a heavy dressing of rotted manure at the rate of about twenty or more loads to the acre. If humus is used, five to ten tons to the acre will give the same result and be longer lasting.

A fairway sixty yards wide and eighty yards long is approximately an acre.

Fairways on Sandy Soils

ON SANDY LOAM, PLOUGHING need not be so deep, but the land will require a dressing of rotted manure or humus, just as much as the clay land.

As drainage of this soil is by its very nature better, it is not so apt to be sour. So it may not be so imperative to dress with lime. But on general principles, liming is good for practically any soil. I have used it on light, sandy soil with astonishingly good results.

In cases of doubt as to the exact soil constituents, it is better to take the precaution of sending a sample to a qualified expert for analysis. That way, you will secure exact knowledge of the requirements of the soil and, can be guided accordingly.

Proper Turf

UNTIL RECENTLY, IT HAS BEEN thought impossible, almost, to grow on golf courses in this country—particularly inland ones—the dwarf grasses which are so essential for the proper development of putting greens and fairways, and which add so much to the pleasure of the game. Indeed, no attempt was made to sow those grasses. It was simply a question of getting one that would grow quickest and cover the surface—those being such coarse grasses as were used on lawns and hay fields.

Experimental work and experience has taught us that the secret is in the proper preparation of the soil. If this is properly handled, there is not the slightest reason why on inland courses a grass cannot be raised of the very finest quality and endurance.

The dwarf grasses which ought to be sown are rather slow in maturing, and this, if we may call it an objection, creates the impression that the wrong variety has to be selected.

They are mostly all creeping in their habit, and if a little patience is used, they will establish themselves, forcing out the coarser, undesirable varieties.

The desirable grass seeds are more expensive, but what difference is a few dollars amount in the price of seed, compared to the enormous loss that must inevitably result when a poor grade is used?

We can't always take the time to test our samples, and very often, as I have discovered, the mixtures we buy do not come up to the standard of the samples supplied.

We must also remember that it takes a long time for grass seed sown on experimental test plots to develop to such a state that we can say whether it is the proper grass or not.

It is often advisable to buy different varieties separately and mix them yourself. This assures, to some extent, your getting what you pay for.

It is not advisable to sow any one kind of grass exclusively, because on every course conditions so vary that no one kind can be expected to best meet all such varying conditions. If the mixture is composed entirely of high grade grasses, the quality of the turf will not be affected.

You can readily see how this would be, as no two greens have exactly the same exposure, or the drainage alike. Some grasses thrive better in hollows, and others on hillsides.

On the other hand, it would be impractical to say that such and such kind should be used exclusively for hollows and another kind for high spots, for the chances are it would not prove our judgment to be correct.

It is sometimes the desire of clubs to save on the grass seed bill by buying the cheaper varieties, forgetting that they generally grow the coarsest and rankest, necessitating constant mowing.

When the dwarf and more expensive varieties are sown, the mowing cost is very much reduced, and the playing conditions are usually much better.

The extra price of the high quality seeds is, in the first year, more than compensated for by the reduction of labor costs.

Using Old Turf

FREQUENTLY A GOLF COURSE is laid out on a piece of property that has been under pasturage or cropped with hay, and the turf may seem to be in fair condition. In such cases it is often the desire of the committee to bring this turf into golfing shape by simple topdressing and seeding.

It is well to remember that to put the kind of turf usually found in America into good golfing condition by this method takes a number of years, and no little labor.

I have seen scarcely any turf in this country that in its natural state would be at all suitable for such treatment. It is my firm belief that it would be better in most cases to plough under the existing turf and utilize it as fertilizer. For that purpose, it has some value.

Reseed the whole tract with the various species of grasses best adapted to the existing soil and climate conditions, and the results will be worthwhile.

Seeding Putting Greens

DON'T LOSE SIGHT OF our suggestion to prepare the land as long ahead of date of seeding as possible, so that there will be ample chance to work the ground over and kill all weeds that may crop up before preparing the seedbed.

After preparing the soil as advised above, hand-rake thoroughly, leaving no rubbish, weeds or small stones. Then treat the whole green to a foot-treading. This "hand treading," as one of my old foremen used to call it, may seem like superfluous work, but it is decidedly the best treatment. The feel of the human foot detects any softness or depression in the surface which might fail to develop by rolling alone. It is most important that the seedbed be firm and free from any sharp depressions.

After the soil has been thoroughly trodden, hand-rake reverse ways, filling in all depressions that are evident.

A seedbed thus perfectly prepared is now all ready for seeding, either by hand or with the use of a machine. The latter is preferable, as a more even distribution of the seed can be secured. It is always advisable to sow in two directions, one-half the quantity each way, to give a more uniform result.

Of course, the quantity of seed required must depend upon the size of the putting green, but as a guide, say that one sixty-by-sixty yard square would require three bushels.

After seeding is all done, hand-rake the entire green very carefully with short-toothed wooden rakes. If they are not available, buy the ordinary lawn rake, cut half off of each tooth, and then point them.

You will find that such rakes are excellent for covering over seed on putting greens, as they go over the surface lightly and prevent the covering of seeds too deeply, a thing to be guarded against. All that is required is that the seed be slightly below the surface.

Now, complete the work by rolling with a roller weighing about three hundred pounds.

Seeding Tees

THE SAME METHOD CAN BE FOLLOWED in the seeding of tees. It's just as important to have the surface firm on a tee as on a green.

Seeding Fairways

IF YOU WANT A REALLY GOOD JOB, after all dressings are thoroughly incorporated into the soil, hand-rake the whole part to be sown.

If you don't want to do this on account of expense, a brush-harrow can be used and dragged all over those parts in opposite directions.

So that you only have to seed once, do the best job either by hand-raking or hand brush-harrowing. After doing this, send a few men over the ground to pick up all rubbish, small roots and stones that may appear.

We are now ready to sow the seed, using an average of eight bushels to the acre, remembering that the heavier the sowing, the thicker sod you'll get. This sowing is best done by machines. We believe the wheat harrow-type to be one of the best.

After sowing the seed both across the fairway and up and down its length, using half the amount in each direction, then brush-harrow lightly the two ways and finish with a roller.

The very best season of the year to sow grass seed is the fall, but not much later than September 10th. Of course, seeding is determined by locality and temperature. When it comes to the extreme northern states, I have made it a point to seed no later than August 15th.

During the fall of the year we expect a good deal more moisture and the ground is warm. In spring, the ground is cold and you're liable to have dry weather at just the time when the young grass needs moisture the most. I would therefore thoroughly urge that the above preparation be given careful consideration.

Don't Overfertilize

IN ORDER TO SECURE the best results from grass seed sown, we must first of all have a well-drained soil, one rich in plant food.

I am not a believer in the use of too much commercial fertilizer in the preparation of the soil for seeding. There is no doubt that certain fertilizers are necessary, but almost all soils require solid organic matter, or humus, to help good drainage and assist in the desired moisture retention of the soil.

We must not forget that we are preparing for a permanent turf. It's out of the question to, year after year, rotate our crop. I would therefore strongly advise that the preparation of the soil, before seeding, be given close study.

If you are in doubt as to the exact requirements in the form of fertilizers, get your soil analyzed. Do not go by chance.

All greenkeepers know that the time to give grass a good start is in the spring.

Mowing New Turf

WE WILL NOW ASSUME that the newly sown grass is in a condition to be cut. Under no conditions let it grow long and rank before the first cutting, as it saps the vitality of the roots, forming a soft top growth which the mowing machines are apt to pull out instead of clip off.

I have found it helpful to roll the whole of it with a light roller before the mower starts, as there are apt to be slight upheavals which, if not pressed down, will come in contact with the knives of the mower.

On the fairways, if the grass clippings fall off in heavy coatings, see that they are scattered, otherwise it will stifle the young grass and cause it to dry out. Long bamboo rods or birch brooms are very useful for this purpose.

On the putting greens, it is not wise to let the clippings of the first few cuttings lie on the surface. Nor should it be allowed anytime the cuttings are of any considerable length. To prevent this, put on the grass catchers.

After the first few cuttings, it is better not to use the catchers. Let the clippings fall on the green, as they serve a purpose as a mulch, doing their part in conserving moisture, also giving shelter for the roots.

About the time the grass is ready for first cutting, it

may be found necessary to give it a stimulant. The steady development of the grass at this period is of utmost importance, and right here is a good time to prepare and apply a fertilizer.

I cannot overemphasize the importance of fertilizing grass produced from spring sowing. The object is to develop it as fast and as far as possible, so as to fortify itself against the summer drought. A slow-acting fertilizer is therefore not quite so suitable.

Grass produced from fall sowing will not be put to the same severe test, and in that case a slow-acting fertilizer is the one to use.

Mowing Greens

CARELESS MOWING IS VERY OFTEN the cause of an uneven putting surface. If the knives of your mower are not properly set, the tendency will be to bruise the grass and leave stubble, rather than cut it.

Most courses do not allocate quite the same manpower for mowing greens as is used at Pinehurst during tournament time.

I have noticed many times where hand mowers were being used that seemed to me to be much too wide. I believe it is a mistake to use wide machines. From fourteen to sixteen inches is a good width.

Don't let your stationary blade be set so low that it will tear the surface and cause injury to the roots. If you can't cut close enough without such a result, there is something radically wrong with your machine.

I do not think it helps a green to let the grass grow long during the summer. It is quite a common practice to raise the knives during the summer months, but I fail to see any advantage derived from it.

Cut the greens north-to-south and east-to-west on alternate days—and occasionally diagonally across the greens. If you persist in cutting the grass always in one direction it will eventually grow in the direction the mowing is done.

What we aim at is to have the grass grow straight, so as to give an even putting surface from all directions.

I Don't Much Care for Rollers

THERE IS NO OPERATION on the care of courses which has caused so much trouble and evil as injudicious rolling.

It has been the custom, when the lies on the fairways were cuppy or where the putting green surface was uneven, to squash the high parts down to meet the low ones. The result of all this work was that the surface became rather smooth and even, and the committees felt satisfied for the time being with that state of affairs.

But very soon greens and fairways deteriorated. When investigation was made as to the cause, it was found to be almost wholly due to this process of heavy rolling.

It is now thoroughly recognized that instead of rolling down the high parts to meet the low, the proper thing to do is to build up the lower parts to meet the high, by topdressing with compost and seed.

On the putting green, to procure a smooth firm surface and still retain the loose condition of soil, which the health of the roots demands, topdressings of compost, sand and charcoal are used.

The result of this change in method is very evident all over the United States, particularly on heavy clay soils. On courses where it had almost become a fixed belief that no grass could be grown, splendid fairways can be seen, and putting greens of high quality are the rule instead of the exception.

Change That Cup

THIS IS A MUCH MORE IMPORTANT feature of greenkeeping than most greenkeepers realize.

It is the common practice to leave the cup in one place until there is a distinct sign of wear and then, when moved, it is usually placed but a short way from its former position. This is a great mistake.

The cup should be moved often and as far away from its former position as possible. There should never be any signs of wear near the cup. Place it near the outer edges of the green as much as in the center.

Many times, the quality of the holes is improved by doing this.

Don't Ignore Tees

GIVE AS MUCH ATTENTION to tees as you do to a green in
the way of cutting, fertilizing and watering.

The care of the tees is one of the most trying
branches of the greenkeeper's work. It is recognized

*The generous fourth tee at Biltmore Forest Country Club is
benched into a hillside but doesn't look forced.*

that the tees on every course have to stand all kinds of abuse.

There is only one real way to keep tees in good condition, and that is to have plenty of them. There are very few courses properly equipped in this direction.

It is rather a simple matter to renovate tees by turfing almost any time of the year, if there is sufficient room for playing on some others.

There is nothing more attractive on any golf course than a good tee to play off.

It is all very well to advise the greenkeeper to move his tee markers often, which is the proper thing to do. But how can any man move them often on a tee fifteen by fifteen? Or even thirty by thirty?

So the thing to do is to have plenty of grass tees. In fact, it not only adds to the pleasure the player derives from playing on them, but affords the opportunity to vary the length and angle of the holes, adding more interest to the course.

A tee with barely room to swing. Lincoln Park in San Francisco may have an inspired setting, but its tee boxes are no things of beauty.

Replace Those Divots

THE SIGN "REPLACE DIVOTS" can be seen all over every golf course. Yet if one cares to take the trouble to watch players, it is apparent that very few read the signs.

I do not believe that replacing the divot helps in any way to get roots still left in the ground to grow again. That is a work for fall renovation with seed and compost. But replacing the divot does certainly help to make the player feel a certain amount of responsibility in the care of the course.

It is argued that this is part of a caddie's work. That may be so, but I do think it would serve a better purpose if members themselves were compelled to put the turf back. On most courses, caddies are trained to go ahead and watch the ball rather than the player. In which case, it cannot be part of the caddie's work.

Players must remember that when the divot is not replaced, another player's ball may find a resting place in the scrape, with the consequence that it is made twice as large, resulting in a distinct damage to the fairway.

The rule to "Replace Divots" should be strictly observed.

Good and Bad Bunkering

THERE SEEMS TO BE a persistently prevalent idea that in marking out a course for bunkering, it is done so as to punish the high-handicap man. This is not so.

If rightly bunkered, the high-handicap man can always find his way to the hole with but little difficulty, provided he uses his brain a bit. But the type of player who depends all on brawn rather than some on brain will find any bunkered course difficult.

In bunkering a course, the aim should be to lay them out so there will be both an easy and a difficult way to each hole. If any player takes the difficult way and is successful, it is only fair that he should have an advantage commensurate with the chance taken and the skill he has shown in playing the stroke.

In any event, the short player will always have his game as a handicap, so it is not consistent to take his game as a standard for which bunkering should be planned.

Here is a thing to remember in constructing your course: It is always advisable to have a number of bunkers marked out at the beginning of construction

Good bunkering at the twelfth at Salem Country Club. The string of pot bunkers helps in gauging distance, is well drained, and easily maintained.

Bad bunkering at a different hole of similar dimensions. Bunkering for art's sake adds little to playing quality, but much to the maintenance budget.

work, so the material from them can be used economically for filling up holes and thus contribute to the quota of topsoil required. This is yet another reason why you should employ an expert golf architect to lay out your course, so those bunkers can be placed exactly in position, without any alterations necessary later.

Obviously such an expert must have an exact knowledge of construction work, as well as know the game thoroughly.

All other things being equal, a man who knows the game and is proficient in playing it will be in a position to give the most dependable advice. But notwithstanding this self-evident fact, the bunkering of a course is sometimes undertaken by a member of the club who locates and shapes the bunkers for no other reason than to suit his own game.

On the other hand, a competent expert will have no personal motives. He'll simply place the bunkers as he believes to be right.

I must tell you of one instance in my own experience which illustrates the force of my advice. It happened on a course where I was asked to plan the bunkering. On one hole where I had taken particular pains to have wing bunkers placed properly (even to the extent of testing out their position by playing up to the hole from every direction), their placement was roundly criticized by one on the committee. He said they were placed exactly where he always played his ball.

It would have amused you to have heard me laboring in an endeavor to convince him why pits should be placed in just those exact positions, and that no course should, in justice to its club members, be laid out for the accommodation of any one individual's game.

I am happy to say those bunkers were constructed as I planned, and the obdurate member of the committee was later so pleased with them that he claimed a good deal of credit for their placement.

Draining Bunkers

Where the subsoil is gravel or sandy, the drainage question of bunkers is not difficult, as it will occur naturally. But in clay soils it is different, especially as it is not always possible to dig bunkers on sloping ground where the drainage can rather easily be looked after.

I have had good success in bunker drainage by digging, at the lowest point, a dry well five feet deep by three in diameter. At the bottom of this well, I took a crow bar and made holes in which I set charges of dynamite. The explosions opened up seams, greatly assisting in drainage. If you follow this example, fill all those big seams with coarse gravel, then close up the well to within six inches of the top with small rocks, finishing off with clean cinders, over which the sand can be spread.

During the spring of the year, when the rains are heavy, the rush of the water may prevent the bunkers from draining with ease, but under ordinary conditions I have found it eminently satisfactory.

Good sand for bunkering is essential. What can be more detestable than a bunker with a clay bottom? No one would have such a bunker, unless the sand was impossible to get because of prohibitive expense. In such a case, a deep grass depression is preferable.

Blasting

DURING CONSTRUCTION, the use of dynamite will be found necessary. Just when and where it shall be used must logically be left entirely in the hands of the man constructing the course.

It is often used effectually in blasting out ditches. In such a case, the line of the ditch would be marked out, and if through clay soil, a crow bar used to punch out blasting holes. Then lay the dynamite and explode several charges at once. It is astonishing what an amount of material can be moved in this way at a very low cost.

It can also be employed in blasting out bunkers in heavy clay or hard subsoil. It is particularly helpful in assisting drainage, as it opens up crevices.

Let me pass along the usual caution that great care must be taken in employing parties to do the work, as it is rather dangerous work, and some of those who have grown accustomed to it are apt to become careless.

Blasting during the construction at this seaside course was mistaken by some in the neighborhood as a naval artillery engagement.

The Need for Water

OVER IN ENGLAND AND SCOTLAND it has recently been found necessary to install water systems to keep their putting greens up with the standard of excellence required in present-day golfing. How much more, then, do we need such systems in America, where we have such droughts?

I remember very well when employed as a greenkeeper at Dornoch Golf Club in Dornoch, Scotland, it was not thought necessary to use water on the greens. Now that a system has been installed, they are able to keep them in a far higher state of excellence. Mr. John Sutherland, the secretary of the club, tells me the watering system has been invaluable in raising the standard of the greens and in keeping them uniformly excellent.

Providing a water supply should be one of our first undertakings, so as to prevent the possibility of losing the grass on the greens after all the seeding expense and labor has been expended on them.

In laying out the watering system, it must not be forgotten that the connections should be made so that tees as well as greens can be conveniently watered if necessary. In a number of American clubs, watering systems have been installed that provide sufficient pressure so even parts of the fairways can be watered if required.

It is not necessary to put the pipes below frost, as during the colder months the water in all the pipes will be drained out. One foot deep is sufficient, except in cases where the pipes must pass over sharp hills. Then it is advisable to cut the ditch deep enough to relieve the sudden bend in the pipes, which would otherwise be apt to strip the joint threads or loosen the caulking. With caulked joint pipes, the joints are rather inflexible and the curves should be very easy.

In laying your pipes, don't neglect to furnish ample drainage basins at all low points so the entire system may be thoroughly drained during the late fall, to prevent the damage of bursting pipes in the winter.

The ideal water is that secured from a pond or brook, provided its supply is dependable throughout the season. The water from such a source is soft and warm, while with artesian wells it is apt to be hard and cold.

The cheapest supply is that furnished by a tank and water ram, the power of which is reckoned approximately eight feet of rise for every foot of fall. When the use of a ram is not practical, then a gasoline or electric pump can be used. The water tank should be erected at the highest point on the ground to secure the necessary pressure.

Sometimes tanks so placed would be a disfigurement to the property, so an air pressure system with an underground tank becomes a happy solution. Such systems are so arranged that both the quantity of water and amount of air pressure is automatically kept constant by a gasoline or electric pump.

In some situations a direct connection to the city water supply, if available, is advisable. But before doing this, it is well to consider the possibility of being either cut off or limited in supply during times of water shortage due to protracted drought. This is sure to occur at just the time when your course most needs water.

So all things considered, it is best to own your own water supply.

Don't Overwater

THERE ARE AS MANY PUTTING GREENS ruined by over-watering, as under.

The recognized principle which should be followed is to water thoroughly and not too often, rather than watering lightly and very often.

In my work on many courses, I have learned two things on greens which have been kept soggy and overwatered: Weeds grow more freely, and there is a greater tendency of winter-kill. Because of excessive watering, the roots do not have the vigor and resistance required to withstand the winter frosts.

Greens underwatered, of course, will have a rather brown appearance during the summer, but it does not follow that because they look slightly brown, they are beyond recovery. To the contrary, it will be found that such greens during the fall and spring are in a very healthy and vigorous condition.

I realize the difficulty that greenkeepers and chairmen of the green committee have in letting up on the watering. Criticism comes from members when they see the slightest sign of a brown patch. Nevertheless, while I do not think it is wise to let a green go completely out of playing condition during the summer, it would be advisable not to overdo the watering of greens during those months.

A very satisfactory way to handle the watering on an eighteen-hole course is to take six greens on the same night and water thoroughly, the second night the second six; the third night the third six, and then return to the first six. In this way, the greens will have sufficient water, and the two days' rest which each green has will be enough to encourage the roots to go downward for the moisture and promote vigorous growth.

It has been found that during the summer months, fairways get in such poor condition on account of droughts, and the playing length and quality of the course is so changed, that watering those parts has become almost a necessity.

It is, of course, a very expensive luxury, and such a system can only be installed by clubs having large money resources.

Temporary irrigation is one way to make certain a green won't be overwatered.

Don't Handicap the Architect

ABOUT A YEAR AGO I was asked to lay out a golf course in the middle west. Before starting the work, a consultation with the board of directors was in order. At this consultation the chairman explained to me what his wishes were. "Now Mr. Ross, we don't want a professional course." My reply was, I don't know what a "professional course" is.

He then said, "What we want is a businessman's course." And my answer was, I don't know what a "businessman's course" is. I only know what a good, bad and indifferent golf course is, and in my work I would try to give them a good course.

Actually, I knew very well indeed what he meant by a "professional" and a "businessman's" course, but with the idea of giving to the club the best their land offered, I did not wish to be hampered. It's a great mistake to undertake to handicap a golf architect in any such fashion.

Let me add that the golf course was laid out as planned, and it is a good one. Our friend, the chairman, says so. There is no member of the club more pleased than he.

Skokie

I FIRST OFFERED THIS following the 1922 U.S. Open at Skokie Country Club:

It is not the best of championship tests, but was not built with that in view. It was built as a golf course on which the members could enjoy their golf, and a delightful course it is to play, but I do not consider it, or for that matter, hardly any of the courses in the country today, outside of Pine Valley, the National and Lido, real championship tests.

For a championship course today would mean a distance of between 6,500 and 7,000 yards, and not five golfers in a thousand want that kind of course for everyday play.

Aronomink

I INTENDED TO MAKE this course my masterpiece, but not until today did I realize I built better than I knew.

Inverness

INVERNESS IS A FINE CHAMPIONSHIP LAYOUT, not as difficult as Interlachen, but provides a good test of golf.

Seminole

IN THESE DAYS OF STEAM SHOVELS and modern improvements, it is possible to do wonderful things on flat, level country.

I have come to the conclusion that I prefer to lay out a course on level land.

The Seminole course near Palm Beach is an example of what can be done with that type of terrain.

I don't say it is the best I have ever designed. Nevertheless, I like it very much.

Oakland Hills

I RARELY FIND A PIECE OF PROPERTY so well-suited for a golf course. Its topographical formation could hardly be surpassed, and the area available is so extensive that I was able to lay out a very open and roomy course. The soil is of sandy loam quality, the very best kind for developing a golf turf.

The course has holes of every type and length. In playing it, all kinds of shots will be demanded. On account of the rolling character of the fairways, the player will be confronted with varying instances demanding perfect control of the strokes to get satisfactory results. The total length of the course for tournament play will be about 6,620 yards, and for general play, 6,400.

It is laid out so that the first tee, ninth green, tenth tee and eighteenth green are all close to the clubhouse. In my first plan, I had arranged for a variety of tees at each hole. I was aware that the USGA had under consideration the changing of the par distance, and I took precautions in planning the holes so that they could be lengthened to the distances required under the new ratings. On my last visit, I planned extra tees on holes numbers two, five, eight, ten, fourteen and eighteen, so that those holes, in addition to number twelve, are par 5s, making the par out 37, in 38, for a total of 75.

Approach shot to the par-4 sixteenth at Oakland Hills. The bold take the long carry directly at the green. The less skilled try the shorter carry well to the left, then play to the green with their third.

Pinehurst

PINEHURST WAS ABSOLUTELY the pioneer in American golf. While the game had been played here in a few places before Pinehurst was established, it was here on these sandhills that the first great national movement in golf was started.

Men came here, took lessons, bought a few clubs, and went away determined to organize courses. They were men of influence in their communities. Their influence gave golf the sort of start it needed in many communities.

This resort, which has long been recognized for its leading influence in golfing circles, took another great step forward in golf in the summer of 1935. The changes which have brought about this great transformation in Pinehurst golf are the entire elimination of sand greens and the substitution of grass putting surfaces on Number Two Course, and the complete remodeling of the layout of this course.

I should like to give you a brief account of the history and the thought that are behind these changes.

First, with respect to the grass greens, for thirty-five years we had been experimenting at Pinehurst with the problem of satisfactory grass surfaces for golf that would be suitable under our climatic and soil conditions. At first it was a question only of fairways, and many grasses were tested until Bermudagrass was selected as the solution, recently improved upon by adding ryegrass in the fall, once a watering system for the fairways was installed.

Next, the clay tees were eliminated and a substitution made of Bermudagrass as a base with rye and redtop filler. This was a great forward step, and led to the use of the same treatment around the sand putting surfaces and finally, with experience and knowledge gained from further experiments, to the use of this method for the entire putting surface.

One summer, three of these greens were built, and because they received the highest commendations from the foremost amateur and professional players, we knew that the problem was solved. We proceeded the next summer with the installation of grass greens on every hole of the Number Two Course.

The story may seem simple in the telling, but much labor and thought, and many disappointments, are also a part of the picture. To attain the high standards which I consider essential for Pinehurst golf, it has been necessary to establish an expensive soil nursery and to develop other features which do not meet the eye of the golfer who enjoys these improvements.

Now, as to the layout, you will at once appreciate that sand greens, which must be flat, seriously limit the architectural features of a golf course. Fortunately, as sand is the ideal soil for a golf course and at Pinehurst we had an especially suitable sandy soil, now we have fine putting surfaces available. We were also able to handle the greens and approaches in ways that would otherwise not have been possible, such as the creation of hollows and contouring that would present impossi-

Your author hitting an approach to one of the new grass greens at Pinehurst No. 2.

ble drainage problems in anything but a natural sandy soil.

Number Two Course has always been a pet of mine, and in building these fine new greens I have been able to carry out many of the changes which I have long visualized but until recently had been unable to put into practice.

I shall speak now only about the course as played from the championship tees, and am disregarding those many features of its design which have to do with the golfer of less than championship ability.

It is obviously the function of a championship course

to present competitors with a variety of problems that will test every type of shot a golfer of championship ability should be qualified to play. Thus, it should call for long and accurate tee shots, accurate iron play, precise handling of the short game, and finally, consistent putting.

These abilities should be called for in a proportion that will not permit excellence in any one department of the game to largely offset deficiences in another. Likewise, penalties must be provided to exact a toll from those who make mistakes and yet, those penalties should not be unduly severe nor of a nature that would prohibit a full recovery by the execution of an unusually well-played shot.

I have said that the tee shot must be long and accurate. A tee shot may be penalized by narrowing the area into which the longer player is hitting, or by giving him an advantage for the second shot, according to the placement of the tee shot.

A good example of the first type of play is the eleventh hole. The bunker on the left side of the fairway will not bother the shorter hitter from the back tee, but by narrowing the fairway, this bunker makes the tee shot more exacting for the longer player, who tries through his length to gain some advantage for the second shot.

Number eight is a fine example of the second type. Here there is a ridge in front of the green which throws a ball played on the right side still further to the right and vice-versa. If the pin is on the right of this green, a player who wishes to avoid the effect of this slope must place his tee shot on the right side of the fairway, and conversely, on the left side of the fairway when the pin is on the left. A majority of the two-shot holes on Number Two are of this general type.

I consider the ability to play the longer irons as the supreme test of a great golfer. That is the ultimate test of a golfer's skill. A golfer who is playing his long irons well will benefit in competitions at Number Two.

Take, for example, the second shot on the fifth hole. The competitor who has elected to play on the left side of the fairway has the opportunity of slapping a boldly-played, high-carrying iron directly on the pin, but certain trouble awaits him on the right, left or short, if he fails to properly execute this shot. The player on the right has a somewhat longer second, and the slope of the green, being more away from him, is therefore likely to undertake an iron shot with lower trajectory. The curl of the green to the left will, however, certainly bring him grief unless he places his shot with fine accuracy or plays with a slight fade.

In the design of the shorter holes designated for irons and chip shots, the Pinehurst conditions offered a really exceptional opportunity. Only in a sandy soil would the drainage problem permit construction of the rolling contours and hollows natural to the Scottish seaside courses where golf was born. This contouring around a green makes possible an infinite variety in the requirements for short shots that no other form of hazard can call for.

I am sure if you watch tournament play on Number Two, you will be interested to see how many times competitors whose second shots have wandered a bit will be disturbed by these innocent-appearing slopes.

Finally, as to the putting, for winter play the greens on this course must be large, and some premium had to be placed on accurate play to the greens. Contours and slopes have consequently been used to break up the greens, which are designed to always give the player near the cup an opportunity for a one-putt, but have minimized the opportunity to get down in less than the regulation number for the golfer whose play to the green has been less accurate.

The sixteenth hole is a fine example of what I have in mind. Here the slope rises gently on the front part of the green and falls slightly away at the rear. Regardless of where the pin may be placed, a player whose approach is either short or strong will be faced with the problem of putting across the ridge formed by this change in slope.

Pinehurst Number Two is the kind of course where every bunker could be removed and you'd never know it.

Bearing in mind that golf should be a pleasure and not a penance, it has always been my thought to present a test of the player's game; the severity of the test to be in direct ratio with his ability as a player. I carried out this thought in the changes made on Number Two.

The expert players will find it one of the longest and most testing courses of their knowledge, for with the added distance has gone hand in hand a remodeling of the bunkering. The end sought was to narrow the fairways by increasing the hazards out where the long hits go, so that the smashing hitters must have accuracy to gain the full benefit of their distance and the shorter hitters may rejoice in the knowledge that they will have broader space in which to land their tee shots.

Players of lesser skill who use the Number Two Course will be glad to know that there are different sets of tees whereby the playing distance has a range from the maximum of 6,900 yards down to 6,200.

As a result of extensive changes, I am firmly of the opinion that the leading professionals and golfers of every caliber, for many years to come, will find in the

The old first at Pinehurst, with a flat, oiled-sand green, girdled by collar of short grass and backed by rough of sand and wire grass.

Number Two Course the fairest yet most exacting test of their game, and yet a test from which they will always derive the maximum amount of pleasure.

This, to my mind, should be the ideal of all golf courses.

*The new first at Pinehurst, with a carpet of Bermuda rumpled
into interesting contours. The short collar and wire grass rough
remain.*

Dornoch

MODESTY FORBIDS ME SAYING more than it is the most beautifully situated links in the world, and that no American golfer should omit to go there, where he will find the best golf, a royal welcome and no rabble.

Greenkeeping versus Club Professionals

GREENKEEPING IS DESTINED TO BE a very important and lucrative profession, of really far greater importance to a golf club than the services of a club professional.

We haven't realized this sufficiently here yet, but already some of the universities in the east have started special courses of greenkeeping and course maintenance.

The Return of Shotmaking

THE NEW STANDARD GOLF BALL has eliminated from the top-notch ranks the mechanical golfer of the past and the skilled shotmaker will now reap his deserved reward. The game was becoming too stereotyped with the old ball. The former ball did not place enough of a premium on a well-hit shot. The sluggers were getting such distances off the tee that they had nothing but easy pitches for second shots. Once they perfected this one method of approach, they scored consistently well.

With the present ball, the skilled shotmaker can play golfers who have the ability to hit long tee shots and then hit their next shot by merely judging the distance and using the required club. I have seen most of the top-ranked golfers at Pinehurst this winter, and the ones who are winning titles now are adjusting their game to fit the changed conditions. On the other hand, some of the amateurs who formerly played in the 70s at Pinehurst were in the 80s this winter because they really were not top-notch golfers and the new ball showed up their deficiencies.

You know, it is one thing to go out and hit every shot

Your author congratulating a true shotmaker, Ben Hogan, upon his victory in the 1942 North & South Open at Pinehurst. He shot a record 271.

the same, merely using a different club for the various distances, and still another to play the shot as it should be played. In the old days we did not have the dozen different irons the present golfer carries. We played with one wooden club, a mid-iron, a mashie, a niblick and a putter. The exact distance from the green did not always determine the club to use. We all learned to play several types of shots with each of these clubs. We had no matched set with numbers determining the club to use.

The new ball will accomplish its purpose if the

golfers will just give it a trial. At present, they are using it as an alibi. They are kidded into thinking that they were 75 shooters because the old ball did not penalize sufficiently their half-missed shots. These same golfers today cannot break 80 because they are mechanical golfers. Instead of trying to perfect their game, they blame the ball. It's easier.

The larger ball also shows up the poor putter. The old ball could be cut or stabbed without affecting its course, and if it was started on line it usually dropped. The new ball must be stroked perfectly to get results.

This ball is also affected more definitely by conditions. Against the wind, in a crosswind, or in a following wind, the ball will act differently, and it is necessary to use some judgment to play this ball.

The new ball will greatly affect the teaching of the game. The young professionals who have not learned the various shots will be greatly handicapped in their teaching. The old-timer, who once had to play all the shots and knows how to teach them, will be in great demand as soon as it is discovered that it is necessary to hit the ball in more than one way.

The new ball has raised the standard of the game, and those with the ability to become skillful will be rewarded for their efforts in the joy of their accomplishment.

The golfer with one shot in his bag will get nowhere in the future.

The Game Is Easier Today

THE GAME IS EASIER NOW. We never used to find two greens on a course that putted alike. No attempt was made in the old days to build a green so that it would hold an approach shot. We never had more than seven clubs, and they were crude compared with the clubs used today.

But the improvements have made the game easier and more attractive for the average player, and that's as it should be.

There has been great progress in golf in recent years, as in every other phase of American life. That's only natural. Look at the time and study the professionals give to the playing of golf today.

The only evil that's creeping into the game, as I see it, is the tendency to bet on it. I don't mean a quarter nassau bet between two friends. What I dislike are the big Calcutta pools. They don't belong in such a fine, clean game.

The original greens at Pinehurst were clay sprinkled lightly with sand. Cracks in the earth were among the obstacles to overcome when putting.

Spoiled Golfers

I'VE BEEN ASKED MY OPINION of the latest generation of golfers.

These young fellows are so completely wrapped up in getting a little golf ball into a little hole in fewer strokes than anyone else that their attitude and sense of intelligent balance to the more important things in life have not only become distorted, but are practically nonexistent.

These boys acquire the idea that golf, or tennis for that matter, is terribly, terribly important. They read about themselves in the sports pages and they become complacent and eager for more and greater laurels.

What is happening is that you cannot carry on an intelligent conversation with most of these big-name youngsters. Sooner or later the talk backfires to golf. Now, golf is a fine game. I would be the last man to say it wasn't. It has been my relaxation and livelihood ever since I was a little shaver in Scotland. But when the game of golf becomes so all-important and feverish and holier than anything else in life, then parents might do worse than turn their young careerists over their knees and administer an old-fashioned spanking.

The young man careerists are not the only offenders. The young lady careerists are just as bad. I see it happen so often that I honestly begin to wonder whether these privileged young people ever get around to reading a newspaper—with the exception of the sports pages. I wonder if they bother to read a good book, or whether they have the faintest conception of labor problems and such things in America.

Who Needs a Golf Course Critic?

THE BRITISH ARCHITECT OF GOLF LINKS pays little heed to criticism, but is open to valuable suggestions, knowing that the carping critic is usually a very ignorant man, while the one who has any advice worth taking gives it in the gentlest way.

No two experts ever agree exactly on points of golf construction, and the best links usually are the outcome of a compromise of ideas gathered from many intelligent sources.

For instance, they do not lay out a links across the water by rule of thumb of having the drive such a distance, the second shot such a distance, the approach such a distance and so on, let alone mentioning the clubs that shall be used for each shot.

When the British architect lays out the hole, he casts his eye over the country and gets the idea of what he considers a golf hole in his brain, lays it out that way, and then says to the player: "There's the golf hole. Play it any way you please!"

As an illustration, take a hole at North Berwick where the majority of good players play an iron shot first, then a full shot with a wood, and then an approach to the green.

An American golfer might say that that was all wrong, as the hole should call for a full shot first, but upon examination there is no reason why such a theory should prevail.

The British one surely has the real spirit of golf in it when it says that the way to reach a hole is by using the clubs and by taking the route which will get the player to the green in his own way. Which should be better for him than anybody else's way.

The golf holes on the best links in Scotland and England have several different ways of playing them, and because they do not present just one and only one way to everybody, the interest in the game increases with the diversity of its problems.

Public Golf

THERE IS NO GOOD REASON why the label "a rich man's game" should be hung on golf.

The game had its origin with the shepherd, who used his crook and a ball to while away the time while the sheep grazed. In my own native country, the shop workers and mill workers throng the links, for which their annual dues amount to about fifty cents, and their total annual expenditures to not more than $5. On account of climatic conditions and greater initial expense, it could hardly be expected that the average cost would be quite so small in this country, but it need not be made greater than the purse of any man could afford.

The development of municipal golf courses is the outstanding feature of the game in America today. It is the greatest step ever taken to make it the game of the people, as it should be. The municipal courses are all moneymakers, and big moneymakers. I am naturally conservative, yet I am certain that in a few years we will see golf played much more generally than is even played now.

I also see a brilliant future for the pay-as-you-enter golf courses of America, a tremendously big new industry.

It's something between a municipal and a country

club golf course. We pick out the land. We let the local men interested in the idea of golf for the people buy a certain percentage of the stock. They eventually may take it over. We are talking about nine-hole courses, which would cost $50,000 or $65,000 with a clubhouse included, a good nine-hole course, too. And we are talking about eighteen-hole courses on the same scale, where good, sporty, attractive layouts may be developed.

There is such a course down in Brockton, Massachusetts, and it could not begin to handle all those who wished to play this past season. Oh, yes, it was a moneymaker. I tell you all such courses are moneymakers. One in Providence has done very well indeed.

Miniature golf courses have made many thousands eager to play golf who never have played it before. Driving ranges have helped create a demand for the public pay-as-you-play courses of regulation length of which I speak.

The pay-as-you-play golf courses all over the east are doing remarkably big business.

Florida versus California

HAVING BEEN IDENTIFIED WITH GOLF in Florida for a number of years, I am frank to say that Florida does not compare with California for golfing advantages, natural and climatic. In California, they have all kinds of most enviable golf territory and can play every day in the year. In Florida, our season is only from November to May first.

But if I may be allowed to say so, we've made much more of our golf attractions in Florida than appears to be done in California.

Let me narrate my own personal experience. I arrived in Los Angeles and, of course, wanted to get a glimpse of the golfing conditions. At the information bureau in the hotel where I was staying, I could get no information whatever as to how I must proceed if I wanted a game of golf. I was referred to one of the gentlemen at the front desk, and all the information he could vouchsafe me was that it would be necessary for me to secure a guest card at one of the clubs, and I must know some member to get the introduction.

So that was, I must infer, a typical reception of a

golfing tourist in southern California. Happily, I subsequently got on the right track, met an old Scottish friend who showed me the courses of the Los Angeles Country Club, Wilshire, Annandale, Pasadena and Rancho Golf Club.

Now, to be still quite frank with you, we do things very differently in Florida. There is not a golfer in the country who is not informed of the golfing advantages at Palm Beach and half a dozen other going resorts in the South. There is a chain of hotels that maintains first-class courses and, believe me, from the moment a traveler starts off from anywhere in the East with a bag of clubs in his luggage, that golfer is going to be drawn toward Florida, if we can do it. And when he once starts toward Florida, he is taken the best care of, supplied with every detail of information and accommodations.

I have no doubt whatever that California is going to be the golfing Mecca of the world, but it does not seem to me that the Californians are in any hurry to realize their great advantage.

California, it seems to me (after a very brief experience, I admit), is neglecting one of its greatest and ripest opportunities.

I am quite convinced of two things:

First, that golf is destined to be the most popular game in the United States, for already more men and women are playing golf than any other game.

Secondly, that California should be the greatest resort of around-the-year golf in the world.

Are British
Courses Better?

THE DISTINCT CHARM of British golf courses lies in their environment and natural attractions. In the first particular, they possess something we cannot hope to rival: a certain sense of fitness, which harmonizes with the ancient Scottish game.

From the latter, however, we can certainly learn much by making our courses less artificial, for the fascination of the most famous hazards in the world lies in the fact that they were not and could not have been constructed.

I avoid the use of the word "created" because a real hazard is and must be a creation of nature.

It is trite to state that anything we have done as course architects in this country—much of which has been criticized as radical in the extreme by home players—does not hold a candle to the work of our continental cousins. Perhaps the best evidence of the modern development of the game are the changes which have made courses more severe and therefore better tests, for golf is not golf when poor play is not penalized. Gradually, criticism of these changes has become fainter and fainter, and time alone is needed for the last vague murmur to be forgotten. One might almost say that changes which were not criticized were inadequate.

The most famous holes of the world are not holes which the novice will enjoy playing and yet, strange as it may seem, this sort of course is exactly the sort of course the novice insists upon playing.

One thing that struck me as extremely queer on my latest trip to Britain was that the average standard of play on the other side seemed vastly inferior to the average standard on this. British golfers seemed to take less pains and to care much less whether they win than in America. Possibly, this is because the larger leisure class has been less under the strain of professional and business life and therefore less sensitive to success or failure. In any event, as I went from one golfing resort to another, I wondered increasingly whether it would be possible to find so many players anywhere in the United States who would so promptly be rated as duffers.

Nevertheless, these duffers were enjoying the game on some of the hardest links to play properly in the world, and woe to the one who should suggest to them that they might find more pleasure on an easier and inferior course.

Behind the Scene
on a Project

HERE WERE MY THOUGHTS as I was laying out Bob
O'Link Golf Club in Chicago:

Taking this land as it lies, it is not hilly like Skokie
or Exmoor. Looking out from the site of the clubhouse,
it appears flat, but walking over it, the course appears
generally rolling and one of the best natural pieces of
golf land I ever worked. The turf is good; will require
ploughing only before the greens, in most cases, to
bring it up to standard.

To begin with, I walked over the land with a sketch-
book in hand for two days before laying a stake. I
could see propositions here and there, but I had to be
cognizant of such things as these:

    – alternating holes with the wind. The prevailing
    winds in the section throughout the summer are in
    the southwest. You can see sleeping porches on
    nearly every home out here facing in that direction.
    With that fact in mind, we must lay out a course
    that will place the wind different on each succeed-
    ing hole;

- taking advantage of the lay of the land for long and short holes. There must be short holes and long holes and medium holes. Each must present its own problems;
- presenting every possibility as I saw them. One of the main things to get away from is the cut-and-dried idea of having one parallel hole after another;
- wasting no ground;
- making no holes overlap or conflict;
- staking out my hazards with an eye toward their usefulness, not only on one hole, but as help for another. It must not simply be a case of teeing up a ball and driving it into space. The bunkers must lie in such a position that the player must think on every shot and figure out how he is going to play it for the fewest possible strokes.

The course must be a pleasure to golfers, rather than a monotony. Putting greens must not be flat and regular. They, too, must present their puzzles. The putt must be just as much a reason for study as the drive or pitch.

Years ago, I started making irregularly-shaped tees. This idea, too, helps in making the course something different.

I do not believe in making a course too hard. That is quite easy to do. I believe a course should be laid out in such a manner that the good short golfer can get to the green quite as well as the long hitter. You know, the average player is the man whose game ranges between 90 and 108, and he has to be taken into consideration.

Taking it all around, the demand today for up-to-date golf courses contains these points:

- It must be a sporty course, not an easy drive, pitch and putt affair;
- It must be as scenic as possible;
- The hazards should be real, not merely holes cut in the ground here and there and banked, or ditches dug, or streams deflected;
- Trees must be removed where they interfere, but so many must not be taken away as to spoil the beauty of the course;
- Above all, it must be a test of the best golf a player is capable of.

Do Golfers Need Rules?

GOLF IS THE ONE GENTLEMAN'S GAME. For this reason, you can never draft rules to control the game completely.

Every golfer is on his honor.

As long as we keep golf a game of honor, we are on the right road.

The game does more to bring out the finer points in a man's character than any other sport. In all my experience at Pinehurst, I know of only two instances of a golfer cheating, only two out of hundreds of thousands. The caddies there have the same high standards of honor.

A country which gets golf-minded need not worry about the honor, the integrity and the honesty of its people.

One Rule That Is Necessary

THE RULE RESTRICTING A PLAYER to fourteen clubs had to be made.

If a player gets the notion the more clubs he carries, the better golf he is going to play, there never would be a limit. In due time, pack mules would have replaced caddies.

As it was, the caddies of the nation were all getting humpbacked, staggering along under freight car loads.

I've been playing golf for more than fifty years, and I don't believe there ever was a round in which I used more than six clubs.

Today, there's a stick in the sack for every shot. If it's a long shot, the stick is there. If it's a short shot, it's there, and if it's an in-between shot, it's there.

In the old days, the player had to make a number of shots with the same club, half-shots, three-quarter shots, and so forth. I doubt that there are a half dozen players today who can bring off fractional shots with any degree of confidence.

I don't say this in criticism. It hasn't been necessary

In the old days, club selection was based on feel, not numbers.

for them to develop these shots. They've had clubs which are designed to make the shots for them.

Golfers used to be made on the golf courses. Now they are made in the machine shops.

Why I Don't Gamble

I USED TO BE APPRENTICED to Old Tom Morris at St. Andrews. Old Tom used to say, "Why make a horse race out of a grand game like golf?" I've always felt that way, too. Golf is too good a game to go out for gambling purposes. You go out for the enjoyment of the game and the company, and not for the money which you may win at it.

Why would anyone make golf into a horse race?

My Debt to the Game

IT IS VERY SATISFYING to be connected with golf. I feel happy to realize that it is to be one of the country's biggest industries, shortly. For I believe wholeheartedly in golf.

I owe the game a great deal, and the way I can repay my debt is by helping to keep it the finest game in the world.

I am not much of a writer.
I find my thoughts run far ahead of my hand and
fingers when I sit down to write.

Donald J. Coss.

A List of Prominent Golf Courses Designed by Donald J. Ross Golf Course Architect

Alabama
Country Club of Birmingham
    Birmingham (East Course, 1927)
    (West Course, 1929)
Country Club of Mobile
    Mobile (1928)
Mountain Brook Club
    Birmingham (1929)

California
Peninsula Golf & Country Club
    San Mateo (Remodeled nine & added nine, 1923)
    (This was formerly Beresford Golf & Country Club.)

Colorado
The Broadmoor Golf Club
    Colorado Springs (1918. Now parts of both East &
    West Courses)
Lakewood Country Club
    Lakewood (Remodeled, 1916)
Wellshire Golf Course
    Denver (1926)

Connecticut
Country Club of Waterbury
    Waterbury (1926)
Greenwich Country Club
    Greenwich (Remodeled, 1946)
Hartford Golf Club
    West Hartford (1914; Also remodeled fourteen &
    added four, 1946)
Shennecossett Golf Course
    Groton (1916; Also remodeled three, 1919)
Wampanoag Country Club
    West Hartford (1924)

An earthen ramp leads from the thirteenth green at Shennecossett to the fourteenth tee.

Florida
Belleair Country Club
    Belleair (East Course, 1925)
    (West Course, remodeled nine & added nine, 1915)
    (This was formerly Belleview-Biltmore Hotel & Club.)
Belleview Mido Country Club
    Belleair (1925)
    (This was formerly Pelican Golf Club.)
Biltmore Golf Club
    Coral Gables (1924)
    (This was formerly the North Course of Miami Biltmore Golf Club.)
Bobby Jones Golf Course
    Sarasota (British Course, 1927)

Bradenton Country Club
    Bradenton (1924)
Brentwood Golf Club
    Jacksonville (1923)
    (This course has closed.)
Country Club of Orlando
    Orlando (1918)
Daytona Beach Golf & Country Club
    Daytona Beach (South Course, 1922)
Delray Beach Golf Course
    Delray Beach (1923)
Dunedin Country Club
    Dunedin (1926)
Florida Country Club
    Jacksonville (1922)
    (This course has closed.)
Fort Myers Golf & Country Club
    Fort Myers (1928)
Gulf Stream Golf Club
    Delray Beach (1923)
Handley Park Golf Club
    New Smyrna Beach (Nine holes, 1922)
    (This course has closed.)
Hyde Park Golf Club
    Jacksonville (1925)
Keystone Golf & Country Club
    Keystone Heights (Nine holes, 1928)
Lake Wales Country Club
    Lake Wales (1925)
Melbourne Golf Club
    Melbourne (1926)
Miami Country Club
    Miami (Remodeled nine & added nine, 1919; Also
    remodeled, 1939)
    (This course has closed.)

A well-contoured green at Palm Beach Country Club.

New Smyrna Beach Municipal Golf Course
New Smyrna Beach (1922)
Palatka Municipal Golf Course
Palatka (1926)
Palm Beach Country Club
Palm Beach (1917)
Palma Ceia Golf Club
Tampa (Remodeled, 1923)
Palma Sola Golf Club
Bradenton (1924)
Panama Country Club
Lynn Haven (1927)
Ponce de Leon Resort & Country Club
St. Augustine (1916)
(This was formerly the North Course of St.
Augustine Links.)

Punta Gorda Country Club
    Punta Gorda (Remodeled, 1927)
Riviera Country Club
    Coral Gables (1924)
    (This was formerly the South Course of Miami
    Biltmore Golf Club.)
St. Augustine Links
    St. Augustine (South Course, 1916)
    (This course has closed.)
San Jose Country Club
    Jacksonville (1925)
Sara Bay Country Club
    Sarasota (1925)
    (This was formerly Whitfield Country Club and
    later Sarasota Bay Country Club.)
Seminole Golf Club
    North Palm Beach (1929)

The sixth at Punta Gorda.

Timuquana Country Club
　　Jacksonville (1923)
University of Florida Golf Club
　　Gainesville (1921)
　　(This was formerly Gainesville Country Club.)

Georgia
Athens Country Club
　　Athens (1926)
Atlanta Athletic Club
　　Atlanta (Course No. 2, 1923)
　　(This course has closed.)
Augusta Country Club
　　Augusta (Remodeled, 1927)
Bacon Park Golf Course
　　Savannah (1926)
Brunswick Country Club
　　Brunswick (Nine holes, 1938)

Bobby Jones finishing a round at Augusta Country Club.

Par-3 eighteenth at East Lake Country Club, where Bobby Jones learned the game.

Country Club of Columbus
    Columbus (Remodeled, 1925; Also remodeled, 1938)
East Lake Country Club
    Atlanta (Remodeled, 1914)
    (This was formerly Atlanta Athletic Club's No. 1
    Course)
Forest Hills Golf Club
    Augusta (1926)
Gainesville Municipal Golf Course
    Gainesville (Nine holes, 1920)
    (This course has closed.)

Highland Country Club
    La Grange (Nine holes, 1922)
Roosevelt Memorial Golf Course
    Warm Springs (1926)
    (Nine holes of this course have been abandoned.)
Savannah Golf Club
    Savannah (Remodeled nine & added nine, 1927)
Sheraton Savannah Resort & Country Club
    Savannah (1929)
    (This was formerly General Oglethorpe Hotel &
    Golf Club.)
Walthour Golf Club
    Savannah (1928)
    (This course has closed.)
Washington Wilkes Country Club
    Washington (Nine holes, 1925).

Illinois
Beverly Country Club
    Chicago (1907)
Bob O'Link Golf Club
    Highland Park (1916)
Calumet Country Club
    Homewood (1917; Also remodeled, 1922)
Evanston Golf Club
    Skokie (1917)
Exmoor Country Club
    Highland Park (Remodeled, 1914)
Hinsdale Golf Club
    Claredon Hills (Remodeled nine & added nine,
    1913)
Indian Hill Club
    Winnetka (Remodeled, 1914 & 1922)
La Grange Country Club
    La Grange (Remodeled, 1921)

The par-3 twelfth at Beverly Country Club is guarded by both water and sand.

Northmoor Country Club
    Highland Park (1918)
Oak Park Country Club
    Oak Park (1916; Also remodeled, 1924)
Old Elm Club
    Highland Park (1913)
Ravisloe Country Club
    Homewood (Remodeled, 1915)
Skokie County Club
    Glencoe (Remodeled, 1915)

Indiana
Broadmoor Country Club
    Indianapolis (1921)

French Lick has exceptional golfing terrain into which the greens and bunkers fit naturally.

Fairview Golf Club
    Fort Wayne (Nine holes, 1927);
French Lick Springs Resort
    French Lick (Hill Course, 1922)

Iowa
Cedar Rapids Country Club
    Cedar Rapids (1915)

Kansas
Shawnee Country Club
    Topeka (Remodeled nine & added nine, 1924)

Kentucky
Idle Hour Country Club
     Lexington (1924)
     (This was formerly Ashland Country Club.)

Maine
Augusta Country Club
     Manchester (Nine holes, 1916)
Biddeford-Saco Country Club
     Saco (Nine holes, 1922)
Cape Neddick Country Club
     Cape Neddick (Remodeled nine & added nine, 1920)
     (This was formerly Cliff Country Club. Nine holes
     have been abandoned.)
Kebo Valley Club
     Bar Harbor (Remodeled, 1926)
Lake Kezar Country Club
     Lovell (Nine holes, 1924)
Lucerne Hills Golf Club
     Lucerne (Nine holes, 1926)
     (This was formerly Lucerne-in-Maine Golf Club.)
Northeast Harbor Golf Club
     Northeast Harbor (Added nine, 1922)
     (This nine has been abandoned.)
Penobscot Valley Country Club
     Orono (1924)
Poland Spring Golf Club
     Poland Spring (Remodeled nine & added nine,
     1913)
Portland Country Club
     Falmouth (1923)
York Golf & Tennis Club
     York (Remodeled, 1923; Also added third nine,
     1930)
     (The third nine has been abandoned.)

Maryland

Chevy Chase Club
    Chevy Chase (1910)
Congressional Country Club
    Bethesda (Blue Course, remodeled, 1930)
Fountain Head Country Club
    Hagerstown (1926)
    (This was formerly Hagerstown Country Club.)
Indian Spring Golf Club
    Silver Spring (1922)
    (This course has closed.)
Prince Georges Country Club
    Landover (1921)
    (This course, formerly Beaver Dam Country Club,
    has closed.)

Massachusetts

Bass River Golf Course
    South Yarmouth (Remodeled nine & added nine,
    1914)
Belmont Country Club
    Belmont (1918)
Brae Burn Country Club
    West Newton (1912; Also remodeled, 1947)
Charles River Country Club
    Newton Centre (1921)
Cohasse Country Club
    Southbridge (Nine holes, 1916; Also remodeled,
    1927 & 1930)
Cohasset Golf Club
    Cohasset (1922)
Concord Country Club
    Concord (Nine holes 1915, added nine holes
    1928)

Country Club of New Bedford
    North Dartmouth (Remodeled nine & added nine,
    1924)
Country Club of Pittsfield
    Pittsfield (1921)
Ellinwood Country Club
    Athol (Nine holes, 1920)
Essex County Club
    Manchester-by-the-Sea (Remodeled, 1909; Also
    remodeled, 1917)
George Wright Golf Course
    Hyde Park (1938)
Greenock Country Club
    Lee (Nine holes, 1927)
Hyannisport Club
    Hyannis Port (Remodeled & added five holes, 1936)

The gentle opening hole at Brae Burn Country Club.

Tumbling terrain and a platform green at Essex County Club.

Island Country Club
    Martha's Vineyard (1913)
    (This course, formerly Martha's Vineyard Golf
    Club, has closed.)
Kernwood Country Club
    Salem (1914)
Longmeadow Country Club
    Longmeadow (1921)
Ludlow Country Club
    Ludlow (1920)
Merrimack Valley Golf Club
    Methuen (1906)

Nantucket Golf Links
    Nantucket (Nine holes, 1917)
    (This course has closed.)
Newton Commonwealth Golf Course
    Newton (1921)
    (This was formerly Commonwealth Country Club.)
North Andover Country Club
    North Andover (Nine holes, 1920)
Oak Hill Country Club
    Fitchburg (Remodeled, 1921)
Oakley Country Club
    Watertown (Remodeled nine & added nine, 1900)
The Orchards Golf Club
    South Hadley (Nine holes, 1922, added nine,
    1931)
Oyster Harbors Golf Club
    Osterville (1927)
Petersham Country Club
    Petersham (Nine holes, 1922)
Plymouth Country Club
    Plymouth Center (Remodeled nine & added nine,
    1921; Also added third nine, 1929)
    (The third nine has been abandoned.)
Pocasset Golf Club
    Pocasset (1916)
Ponkapoag Golf Club
    Canton (Course No. 1, 1931; Also remodeled,
    1939) (Course No. 2, nine holes, 1939)
Salem Country Club
    Peabody (1925)
Sandy Burr Country Club
    Wayland (1925)
Springfield Country Club
    West Springfield (1924)

Tatnuck Country Club
    Worcester (Nine holes, 1930)
Tedesco Country Club
    Marblehead (Added one hole, 1937)
Tekoa Country Club
    Westfield (Nine holes, 1923)
Toy Town Tavern Golf Club
    Winchendon (1924)
    (This course has closed.)
Vesper Country Club
    Tyngsboro (Remodeled nine and added nine, 1919)
Wachusett Country Club
    West Boylston (Nine holes, 1911)
Waltham Country Club
    Waltham (Nine holes, 1921)
    (This course has closed.)
Wellesley Country Club
    Wellesley (Nine holes, 1911)
Weston Golf Club
    Weston (Nine holes, 1916, added nine holes, 1923)
Whaling City Golf Club
    New Bedford (Nine holes, 1920)
Whitinsville Golf Club
    Whitinsville (Nine holes, 1925)
Wianno Golf Club
    Osterville (Remodeled, 1913; Remodeled nine,
    added nine, 1920)
William J. Devine Golf Course
    Dorchester (Remodeled nine & added nine, 1922)
    (This was formerly Franklin Park Golf Course.)
Winchester Country Club
    Winchester (1903; Also remodeled, 1928)
Woodland Golf Club
    Auburndale (Remodeled, 1928)

The short downhill tenth at Worcester Country Club has bunkers above the surface of the green.

Worcester Country Club
    Worcester (1913)
Wyckoff Park Golf Course
    Holyoke (1923)
    (This was formerly Mt. Tom Country Club.)

Michigan
Barton Hills Country Club
    Ann Arbor (1920)
Bloomfield Hills Country Club
    Bloomfield Hills (Remodeled, 1936)
Dearborn Country Club
    Dearborn (1925)
Detroit Golf Club
    Detroit (North Course 1916; also remodeled, 1936)
    (South Course, 1916)

Elk Rapids Golf Club
  Elk Rapids (Nine holes, 1923)
Franklin Hills Country Club
  Franklin (1926)
Fred Wardell Estate Golf Course
  Detroit (Nine holes, 1920)
  (This course has closed.)
Grosse Ile Golf & Country Club
  Grosse Ile (1920)
Hawthorne Valley Golf Club
  Dearborn (Twenty-seven holes, 1925)
  (This course, formerly known as Brightmoor
  Country Club, has closed.)
Highland Park Golf Club
  Grand Rapids (Remodeled nine & added nine,
  1922)
Highlands Country Club
  Grand Rapids (Added nine, 1927)
  (This course has closed.)
Kent Country Club
  Grand Rapids (Remodeled nine & added nine,
  1921)
Monroe Golf & Country Club
  Monroe (1919)
Muskegon Country Club
  Muskegon (1911)
Oakland Hills Country Club
  Bloomfield Hills (North Course, 1923)
  (South Course, 1917)
Rackham Golf Course
  Huntington Woods (1925)
Rogell Golf Course
  Detroit (1921)
  (This was formerly Redford Country Club.)

A sunken pit on the seventeenth at Oakland Hills Country Club.

Shadow Ridge Golf Club
    Ionia (Nine holes, 1916)
    (This was formerly Ionia Country Club.)
Warren Valley Golf Club
    Wayne (East Course 1927)
    (West Course 1927)
Western Golf & Country Club
    Redford (1926).

Minnesota
Interlachen Country Club
    Edina (Remodeled, 1921)
Minikahda Club
    Minneapolis (Remodeled, 1917)
Northland Country Club
    Duluth (1927)
White Bear Yacht Club
    White Bear Lake (Nine holes, 1912, added nine,
    1915)

Minikahda's first is only 326 yards, but pot bunkers guard the green.

Woodhill Country Club
    Wayzata (1917, Also remodeled 1934)

Missouri
Hillcrest Country Club
    Kansas City (1917)
Midland Valley Country Club
    Overland (1919)
    (This course has closed.)

New Hampshire
Bald Peak Colony Club
    Melvin Village (1922)

A good sunken pit on the tenth at Hillcrest Country Club.

Balsams Grand Resort Hotel
    Dixville Notch (Panorama Course, 1915)
Bethlehem Country Club
    Bethlehem (Remodeled nine & added nine, 1912)
Farnum Hill Golf & Country Club
    Lebanon (Nine holes, 1923)
    (This was formerly Carter Country Club.)
Kingswood Country Club
    Wolfeboro (1926)
Lake Sunapee Country Club
    New London (1928)
Lake Tarleton Club
    Pike (1916)
    (This course has closed.)
Manchester Country Club
    Bedford (1923)
Maplewood Country Club
    Bethlehem (Remodeled nine & added nine, 1914;
    Also remodeled, 1928)

Trees grow in a bunker on this par-3 at Maplewood Country Club.

Mount Crotched Country Club
 Francestown (Nine holes, 1929)
 (This course has closed.)
Mount Washington Golf Club
 Bretton Woods (Remodeled nine & added eighteen, 1915)
Wentworth-by-the-Sea Golf Club
 Portsmouth (Nine holes, 1910)

New Jersey
Crestmont Country Club
 West Orange (1923)
Deal Golf & Country Club
 Deal (Remodeled & added three, 1915)

Echo Lake Country Club
    Westfield (1919)
    (This was formerly Cranford Golf Club.)
Englewood Country Club
    Englewood (Remodeled 1916)
    (This course has closed.)
Essex Fells Country Club
    Essex Fells (1923)
    (This was formerly Newark Athletic Club.)
Homestead Country Club
    Spring Lake (1920)
    (This course has closed.)
Knickerbocker Country Club
    Tenafly (1915)
Lone Pine Golf Club
    New Brunswick (1925)
    (This course has closed.)

A slightly crowned green on the par-4 eighth at Echo Lake Country Club.

Montclair Golf Club
    Montclair (Twenty-seven holes, 1919)
Mountain Ridge Country Club
    West Caldwell (1930)
Plainfield Country Club
    Plainfield (1921; also added three, 1930)
Ridgewood Country Club
    Ridgewood (Remodeled, 1916)
    (The club has abandoned this course for one in
    another town.)
Riverton Country Club
    Riverton (1916)
Marriott's Seaview Resort
    Absecon (Bay Course, remodeled bunkering, 1918)
    (This was formerly Seaview Golf Club.)

New York
Apawamis Club
    Rye (Added three, 1930)
Bellevue Country Club
    Syracuse (1914)
Brook Lea Country Club
    Rochester (1926)
Chautauqua Golf Club
    Chautauqua (Remodeled nine & added nine, 1921)
Country Club of Buffalo
    Williamsville (1926)
Country Club of Rochester
    Rochester (1913)
Chappequa Country Club
    Mount Kisco (1929)
    (This course has closed.)
Elmsford Country Club
    Elmsford (1919)
    (This course has closed.)

Fairview Country Club
    Elmsford (1912)
    (This course has closed.)
Fox Hills Golf Club
    Staten Island (Remodeled, 1928)
    (This course has closed.)
Glenburnie Golf Course
    Lake George (Remodeled & added three, 1915)
    (This course has closed.)
Glens Falls Country Club
    Glens Falls (1923)
Hudson River Country Club
    Yonkers (1916)
    (This course has closed.)
Irondequoit Country Club
    Rochester (Nine holes, 1916)
Mark Twain Golf Course
    Elmira (1940)
Monroe Country Club
    Pittsford (1923)
North Fork Country Club
    Cutchogue (Nine holes, 1912, added nine, 1922)
Oak Hill Country Club
    Rochester (East Course, 1924)
    (West Course, 1924)
The Sagamore Resort & Golf Club
    Bolton Landing (1928)
Siwanoy Country Club
    Bronxville (1914)
Teugega Country Club
    Rome (1920)
Thendara Golf Club
    Thendara (Nine holes, 1921)
Wykagyl Country Club
    New Rochelle (Remodeled, 1920)

The sixth green (foreground) and seventh fairway at The Sagamore.

North Carolina
Alamance Country Club
    Burlington (1947)
Benvenue Country Club
    Rocky Mount (1922; also remodeled, 1946)
Biltmore Forest Country Club
    Asheville (1925)
Blowing Rock Country Club
    Blowing Rock (Remodeled nine & added nine, 1922)
Buncombe County Golf Course
    Asheville (1927)
    (This was formerly Asheville Municipal Golf Course.)
Burlington Country Club
    Burlington (1928)

Cape Fear Country Club
    Wilmington (Remodeled & added seven, 1926; also
    remodeled, 1946)
Carolina Golf & Country Club
    Charlotte (1928)
Carolina Pines Golf Club
    Raleigh (1932)
    (This course has closed.)
Catawba Country Club
    Newton (1946)
Charlotte Country Club
    Charlotte (Remodeled, 1925; also remodeled 1942
    & 1947)
Country Club of Asheville
    Asheville (1928)
    (This was formerly Beaver Lake Golf Club.)
Country Club of Salisbury
    Salisbury (Remodeled, 1927)
Forsyth Country Club
    Winston-Salem (1911)
    (This was formerly Twin City Country Club.)
Greensboro Country Club
    Greensboro (Irving Park Course, 1911)
Grove Park Inn & Country Club
    Asheville (Remodeled, 1926)
    (This was formerly Asheville Country Club.)
Hendersonville Country Club
    Hendersonville (1927)
    (This was formerly Laurel Park Country Club.)
Highland Country Club
    Fayetteville (1945)
Highlands Country Club
    Highlands (1928)
Hope Valley Country Club
    Durham (1927)

Lenoir Golf Club
    Lenoir (Nine holes, 1928)
Linville Golf Club
    Linville (1924)
Mid Pines Golf Club
    Southern Pines (1921)
Mimosa Hills Golf Club
    Morganton (1928)
Monroe Country Club
    Monroe (Nine holes, 1927)
Mooresville Golf Club
    Mooresville (Nine holes, 1948)
    (This was formerly Moore Park Golf Club.)
Myers Park Country Club
    Charlotte (Remodeled nine & added nine, 1930;
    also remodeled, 1945 & 1947)
Overhills Golf Club
    Overhills (Nine holes, 1910; added nine, 1918)
Pennrose Park Country Club
    Reidsville (Nine holes, 1928)
Pine Needles Country Club
    Southern Pines (1927)
Pinehurst Resort & Country Club
    Pinehurst (No. 1 Course, remodeled nine & added
    nine, 1901; also remodeled 1913, 1940 & 1946;
    Major remodeling, 1937)
    (No. 2 Course, nine holes, 1901, added nine, 1906;
    Also remodeled 1923, 1933, 1934 & 1947; Major
    remodeling, 1935)
    (No. 3 Course, nine holes, 1907, added nine, 1910;
    Major remodeling 1936; also remodeled, 1946)
    (No. 4 Course, six holes, 1912, added three 1914,
    added nine, 1919; This course has closed.)
    (No. 5 Course, nine holes, 1928, added nine, 1935;
    This course has closed.)

The par-4 fourth at Pinehurst No. 2 curves along a natural draw.

Raleigh Country Club
    Raleigh (1948)
Richmond Pines Country Club
    Rockingham (Nine holes, 1926)
Roaring Gap Club
    Roaring Gap (1926)
Ryder Golf Club
    Fort Bragg (Nine holes, 1922)
    (This was formerly Fort Bragg Golf Club's Course
    No. 1.)

Sedgefield Country Club
    Greensboro (1926)
Southern Pines Country Club
    Southern Pines (Course No. 1, 1923)
    (Course No. 2, 1928; Nine holes have been
    abandoned.)
Tryon Country Club
    Tryon (Nine holes, 1916)
Waynesville Country Club
    Waynesville (Nine holes, 1924)
Wilmington Golf Course
    Wilmington (1926)

Ohio

Acacia Country Club
    Lyndhurst (1923)
Arlington Golf Club
    Columbus (Remodeled nine & added nine, 1921)
    (This course, formerly Alladin Country Club, has
    closed.)
Athens Country Club
    Athens (Nine holes, 1921)
Brookside Country Club
    Canton (1922)
Columbus Country Club
    Columbus (Remodeled nine & added nine, 1914;
    also remodeled 1920 & 1940)
Congress Lake Club
    Hartville (Remodeled, 1926)
Dayton Country Club
    Dayton (1919)
Delaware Golf Club
    Delaware (Nine holes, 1925)
    (This was formerly Odevene Country Club.)

Elks Country Club
    Worthington (1923)
    (This course has closed.)
Elks Country Club
    McDermott (1920)
    (This was formerly Portmouth Country Club.)
Granville Golf Club
    Granville (1924)
Hamilton Elks Country Club
    Hamilton (1925)
Hawthorne Valley Country Club
    Solon (1926)
Hyde Park Golf & Country Club
    Cincinnati (1927)
Inverness Club
    Toledo (Remodeled nine & added nine, 1919)
Lancaster Country Club
    Lancaster (Remodeled nine, 1926)
Maketewah Country Club
    Cincinnati (1919; also remodeled 1929)
    (This was formerly Hamilton County Golf Course.)
Manakiki Golf Club
    Willoughby (1928)
Mayfield Country Club
    Euclid (Remodeled, 1935)
Miami Shores Golf Club
    Troy (1947)
Miami Valley Golf Club
    Dayton (1919)
Mill Creek Park Golf Club
    Youngstown (North Course 1928)
    (South Course 1928)
Mohawk Golf Club
    Tiffin (Nine holes, 1917)

The steep climb to the green on the par-3 ninth at Scioto.

Oakwood Club
    Cleveland (Remodeled, 1915 & 1920)
Piqua Country Club
    Piqua (Nine holes, 1920)
Scioto Country Club
    Columbus (1916)
Shaker Heights Country Club
    Shaker Heights (1916)
Springfield Country Club
    Springfield (1921)
Westbrook Country Club
    Mansfield (1920)
Willowick Country Club
    Willoughby (Remodeled, 1917)
Wyandot Golf Course
    Centerburg (1922)

Youngstown Country Club
    Youngstown (Remodeled, 1921)

Pennsylvania
Allegheny Country Club
    Sewickley (Added three holes, 1933)
Aronimink Golf Club
    Newtown Square (1928)
Bedford Springs Golf Club
    Bedford (Remodeled nine & added nine, 1924)
Buck Hill Golf Club
    Buck Hill Falls (1922)
Cedarbrook Country Club
    Philadelphia (Remodeled, 1921)
    (The club has abandoned this course for one in
    another town.)
Chester Valley Golf Club
    Malvern (1928)
Country Club of York
    York (1928)

A bunker-mound combination on the fifth at Buck Hill Golf Club.

Edgewood Country Club
    Pittsburgh (1921)
Elkview Country Club
    Carbondale (Nine holes, 1925)
Green Oaks Country Club
    Verona (1921)
    (This was formerly Westmoreland Country Club.)
Gulph Mills Golf Club
    King of Prussia (1919)
Kahkwa Club
    Erie (1918; also remodeled bunkering, 1927)
Kennett Square Golf & Country Club
    Kennett Square (Nine holes, 1923)
Lewistown Country Club
    Lewistown (Nine holes, 1945)
Lu Lu Country Club
    North Hills (1912)
Overbrook Country Club
    Overbrook (Remodeled nine & added nine, 1922)
    (The club has abandoned this course for one in another town.)
Pocono Manor Golf Club
    Pocono Manor (East Course, remodeled, 1919)
Rolling Rock Club
    Ligonier (Nine holes, 1917; also remodeled, 1947)
St. Davids Golf Club
    Wayne (1927)
Schuykill Country Club
    Orwegsburg (Remodeled nine & added nine, 1945)
Silver Creek Country Club
    Hellertown (1947)
    (This was formerly Bethlehem Steel Club.)

Sunnybrook Country Club
    Flourtown (1921)
    (The club has abandoned this course for one in
    another town.)
Torresdale-Frankford Country Club
    Philadelphia (Remodeled nine & added nine,
    1930)
Tumblebrook Golf Club
    Coopersburg (Nine holes, 1931)
Wanango Country Club
    Reno (Nine holes, 1913)
Whitemarsh Valley Country Club
    Lafayette Hill (Remodeled, 1930)

Rhode Island
Agawam Hunt Golf Club
    Rumford (Remodeled, 1911)
Metacomet Country Club
    East Providence (1921)
Misquamicut Golf Club
    Westerly (Remodeled, 1923)
Newport Country Club
    Newport (Remodeled, 1915)
Point Judith Country Club
    Narragansett (Remodeled nine & added nine,
    1927)
Rhode Island Country Club
    Barrington (1912)
Sakonnet Golf Club
    Little Compton (1921)
Triggs Memorial Golf Course
    Providence (1932)
Wannamoisett Country Club
    Rumford (1914; also remodeled, 1926)

The sixth at Rhode Island Country Club.

Warwick Country Club
    Warwick (Nine holes, 1924)
Winnapaug Country Club
    Westerly (Nine holes, 1922, added nine, 1928)

South Carolina
Camden Country Club
    Camden (Remodeled, 1939)
Cheraw Country Club
    Cheraw (Nine holes, 1924)
Fort Mill Golf Club
    Fort Mill (Nine holes, 1946)
    (This was formerly Spring Mill Country Club.)
Lancaster Golf Course
    Lancaster (Nine holes, 1935)

Tennessee
Belle Meade Country Club
    Nashville (1921)
Chattanooga Golf and Country Club
    Chattanooga (1920)
Cherokee Country Club
    Knoxville (Remodeled & added three holes, 1925)
Holston Hills Country Club
    Knoxville (1928)
Memphis Country Club
    Memphis (1910)
Richland Country Club
    Nashville (1920)
    (The club has abandoned this course for one in
    another town.)
Ridgefields Country Club
    Kingsport (1947)
Tate Springs Golf Club
    Tate Springs (1924)
    (This course has closed.)

Texas
Galveston Municipal Golf Course
    Galveston (1921)
    (This course has closed.)
River Oaks Country Club
    Houston (Nine holes, 1924, added nine, 1927)
Sunset Grove Country Club
    Orange (1923)

Vermont
Burlington Country Club
    Burlington (1930)
Woodstock Country Club
    Woodstock (Remodeled, 1938)

Virginia
Army-Navy Country Club
    Arlington (Remodeled, 1944)
Belmont Park Golf Course
    Richmond (Remodeled, 1940)
    (This was formerly Hermitage Country Club.)
Country Club of Petersburg
    Petersburg (1922)
Hampton Golf Association
    Hampton (1930)
    (This was formerly Hampton Roads Golf Club.)
The Homestead Golf Club
    Hot Springs (Remodeled six holes & added twelve,
    1913)
Jefferson-Lakeside Club
    Richmond (1921)
Washington Golf & Country Club
    Arlington (1915)
Westwood Golf Club
    Richmond (Remodeled, 1916)
    (This course has closed.)
Woodberry Forest Golf Club
    Woodberry Forest (Nine holes, 1910).

Wisconsin
Kenosha Country Club
    Kenosha (1922)
Oconomowoc Golf Club
    Oconomowoc (1915).

Alberta
Banff Hotel Golf Course
    Banff Springs (1917)
    (This course has been replaced.)

Manitoba
Elmhurst Golf Links
   Winnipeg (Remodeled nine & added nine, 1923)
 Pine Ridge Golf Club
   Winnipeg (Remodeled, 1922)
   (This course has been replaced.)
St. Charles Country Club
   Winnipeg (Remodeled nine & added nine, 1920)

New Brunswick
Algonquin Hotel & Golf Club
   St. Andrews-by-the-Sea (Seaside Course,
   Remodeled nine & added nine, 1921)
   (Woodland Course, nine holes, 1921)
Riverside Golf & Country Club
   Saint John (Remodeled, 1937)

Nova Scotia
Brightwood Golf & Country Club
   Dartmouth (Remodeled, 1934)
Liverpool Golf Club
   Hunts Point (1928)
   (This was formerly White Point Beach Golf Club.)

Ontario
Bridgewater Golf Club
   Fort Erie (1929)
Essex Golf & Country Club
   La Salle (1929)
Lambton Golf & Country Club
   Toronto (Remodeled, 1919)
Mississaugua Golf & Country Club
   Port Credit (Remodeled, 1919)
Rosedale Golf Club
   Toronto (Remodeled, 1919)

Roseland Golf & Curling Club
    Windsor (Twenty-seven holes, 1921; also
    remodeled, 1924)

Quebec
Kanawaki Golf Club
    Montreal (Remodeled, 1920)
Royal Ottawa Golf Club
    Hull (Remodeled, 1912)

Cuba
Country Club of Havana
    Havana (1911)
    (This course has closed.)
Havana Biltmore Golf Club
    Havana (1927)
    (This course has closed.)

A Caribbean paradise, the Country Club of Havana on the island of Cuba.

Scotland
Royal Dornoch Golf Club
    Dornoch (Remodeled & added two holes, 1921)

Acknowledgments

We are indebted to the following golf course architects who helped with the book: Ron Forse, Dr. Michael Hurdzan, Rees Jones, Stephen Kay, Dan Maples, Brian Silva, David Gordon, John Fought and Phil Wogan; and to the following photographers: Jim Moriarty, Brian Smith and Dean Batchelder. Additional thanks to Karen Bednarsky and the staff of the U.S.G.A. Library and Museum, Far Hills, NJ, Kris Januzik and the staff of the Tufts Archives at Givens Memorial Library, Pinehurst, NC and Gail McGarry, librarian at *Golf Digest* magazine, Trumbull, CT. A special acknowledgment to W. Pete Jones of Raleigh, NC, the official historian for the Donald Ross Society.

Afterword

There are few individuals who, by dint of their personality and creative output, put their imprint on a profession forever.

Donald J. Ross was such a stalwart in golf course architecture.

In 1996, the members of the American Society of Golf Course Architects celebrated the group's 50th anniversary in Ross' beloved Pinehurst, gathering at the Donald Ross Banquet in their Ross tartan blazers after completing their golf competition on three Donald Ross courses! The theme of the meeting, of course, focused on the Grand Master's impact on American golf course architecture.

Ross and the few golf course architects in business after World War II had several informal meetings to discuss the possibility of forming a professional organization, finally deciding to proceed during a meeting in New York. The first annual meeting was hosted by Ross in Pinehurst, so it was fitting for the Society to return for its 50th annual meeting. By acclamation, the charter members elected Donald Ross Honorary President of the newly-formed American Society of Golf Course Architects.

The Society's charter members thought an organiza-

The American Society of Golf Course Architects held its first annual meeting at Pinehurst on December 5, 1947. Shown at that meeting (left to right) are: William P. Bell, Robert White, W.B. Langford, Honorary President Donald J. Ross, President Robert Bruce Harris, Vice President Stanley Thompson, William F. Gordon, Secretary-Treasurer Robert Trent Jones, William Diddel, and J.B. McGovern. Four of the original 14 charter members, Perry Maxwell, Jack Daray, Wayne Stiles, and Robert F. "Red" Lawrence, were not able to attend the first Pinehurst meeting.

tion would help them upgrade the profession and advance new design concepts and construction techniques through collective discussion. Built on this original premise, the Society today has more than 125 members and is an important member of the Allied Associations of Golf.

In his memory, the Society presents the Donald Ross Award annually to an individual who has made a significant contribution to golf in general and golf course architecture specifically. Members of the American Society of Golf Course Architects are proud of their history, and demonstrate that daily by wearing the Ross family tartan blazer as a proud salute to Founding Member and Honorary President, Donald J. Ross.

Paul Fullmer
American Society of Golf Course Architects
Executive Secretary

Photo Credits